DID YOU KNOW...

*Crystal balls really do work...and why?

*Why Ouija boards are too dangerous to use?

*That you can develop not only clairvoyance, but also clairaudience (psychic hearing) and clairsentience (psychic smells)?

*How to correctly interpret dreams of premonition?

*How to spot a case of possession?

*What is the first sign that you have psychic touch—and healing ability?

Let Dr. Richard Lawrence give you answers, and many more techniques, that will heighten your consciousness and spiritual awareness.

**Psychic ability is fun and fulfilling.
And it may be your destiny.**

UNLOCK YOUR
PSYCHIC
POWERS

DR. RICHARD LAWRENCE

SMP
ST. MARTIN'S PAPERBACKS

To His Eminence Dr George King
who has demonstrated what psychic powers can mean
to the world as a whole

First published in Great Britain by Souvenir Press Ltd.

UNLOCK YOUR PSYCHIC POWERS

Copyright © 1993 by Richard Lawrence.

ISBN: 0-312-95412-3

Printed in the United States of America

St. Martin's Paperbacks edition/April 1995

10 9 8 7 6 5 4 3 2

Contents

Publisher's Note

*

This book has been written by a psychic practitioner fully experienced in the techniques of personal and psychic development described herein. It is important, however, that before attempting any of the practices you should read and take note of the correct procedures and of the precautions and warnings given in the text. It is especially important that anyone with a history of mental illness should not try to practise psychic development until he or she has stabilised the condition under the correct medical supervision.

The Publisher makes no representation, express or implied, with regard to the accuracy of the information contained in this book, and legal responsibility or liability cannot be accepted by the Author or the Publisher for any errors or omissions that may be made or for any loss, damage, injury or problems suffered or in any way arising from the uses of any techniques described.

Acknowledgements

*

Special thanks are due to my wife, Alyson, for designing the illustrations; to Pat Higginson, Marjorie Lent and Christopher Perry for their help in preparing the manuscript; and to Dr John Holder and Brian Keneipp for their advice and support throughout the writing of this book.

Preface

*

It was the summer of 1971 during the school vacations, just prior to my first term as a music student at Hull University. I had decided to spend the summer in France, visiting friends and earning money as a pianist. I told my parents I would probably be away for at least two months.

After a month in France, however, I decided to return home early to concentrate on my classical music studies before going up to university. This would be a complete surprise for my parents, who had no contact with me in France and did not know where I was staying.

The boat docked at Dover in the late evening and I managed to hitch a lift to my home town of Sevenoaks in Kent, arriving there in the early hours of the morning. In order not to disturb my parents at this anti-social hour, I planned to camp out in the garden for the night.

It was approximately 3.00 a.m. as I quietly walked up the drive, to find to my amazement that the lights in the house were on and my father was looking out of the window waiting for me. In short, I was expected. My mother had woken some hours earlier and informed my father that I would return that night. In fact, they were somewhat annoyed that I had taken so long!

My mother was not at that time a believer in or practitioner of anything remotely psychic, and yet she had demonstrated her intuitive ability most effectively.

In itself this incident was trifling and of no importance to anyone else. The only practical benefit it brought was that I slept in my room instead of the garden that night. It is, however, typical of thousands of cases experienced by ordinary people from all walks of life—many of which have a far greater significance than this one.

To me, it illustrated something I was already starting to believe: that an innate faculty exists within all of us which is beyond reason—namely the mysterious power of intuition.

Ten years later I had become full-time European Secretary of The Aetherius Society, a New Age organisation devoted, among other things, to the study of paranormal phenomena. Following the premise that the finest form of study is practice, I had embarked on an intensive programme of psychic development under the first-rate guidance of the Society's Founder/President, His Eminence Dr George King.

As part of my duties at that time, I visited a very keen but ageing member of the Society in Switzerland. One evening, as we sat alone discussing metaphysical subjects of mutual interest, I became acutely aware of a third person in the room. His presence was strong and definite, but to my sight apparently blurred. I could discern that he was wearing formal military dress and a dress sword—as though attending an official royal or military function.

To me, at the time, the whole experience was completely natural. A sceptic would say I was 'seeing things', and if no more had happened it would be perfectly reasonable for him to dismiss it as hallucination or pure imagination.

But then the military gentleman spoke to me. Again I must admit that, at that stage in my psychic development, the exact accent and intonation were blurred. The words, though, were absolutely clear. He asked me to go to the bookshelf where I would find an encyclopaedia. He told me to open it at the name Rommel, and to read a particular paragraph aloud.

Embarrassed, yet excited by this experience, I did just that and read out the paragraph to my elderly friend, whose mouth dropped open in astonishment. The paragraph described an incident in which a particular British General had been taken captive by Rommel early in the Second World War. It was not the strategic implications of this defeat that staggered my friend, though—it was the fact that, unbeknown to me, this General, who was named in the text, had been a close relative of his. For confidential reasons I cannot reveal exact names and relationships, but his relative had returned from 'the other side' to prove through this small demonstration that there is no such thing as death. His surname was different from that of my friend and I had no previous knowledge of this side of his family, his mother's side. Further personal messages were passed from one to the other through my psychic intervention—for my friend was not able to see or hear his relative.

This is another personal incident which is one of thousands that happen to people everywhere. Indeed, I have been privileged to experience dozens of cases myself since then, some of which were far more important and just as convincing as this one. So have numerous mediums, psychics and intuitive people from all parts of the world.

Natural as it seemed to me at the time, I must say I had to pinch myself afterwards to see whether I was dreaming. But I realised that I had started to show signs of an ability I had been working to develop for some time—the ability to practise clairvoyance (psychic vision) and clairaudience (psychic hearing). I am convinced that this can be done by anyone who chooses to do so.

These cases are not presented as proof, for they can be dismissed by any sceptic as figments of the imagination. They are proof to no one but me, for I experienced them, and personal experience is the key to understanding psychic development.

The orthodox scientist often dismisses personal testimony as unsubstantiated. Everything must be repeatable under identical physical conditions before he can believe it. And there lies the flaw in his argument. Is the feeling of love repeatable under exactly the same physical conditions? Indeed, is any feeling repeatable under exactly the same physical conditions?

Psychic powers are all about feeling. A mysterious faculty can be awakened through feeling which will help us to read the signs of life and the forces of destiny that govern it.

I

Mysteries of the Mind

*

The exact function of the mind is a constant source of speculation. There is disagreement on a variety of theories from
different academic disciplines and research projects. Some
approach it from a primarily neurological point of view, believing that the entire secret can be revealed by understanding
the function of the brain. Others tackle it from a primarily
psychological point of view, especially taking into account
emotional and subconscious behaviour. Others, drawing upon
a rich fund of teaching, analyse this fascinating subject from
a metaphysical point of view, including in their findings such
concepts as the soul and spirit of man.

An in-depth analysis of the mind is beyond the scope of
this book. We are concerned here with one particular aspect
of its function—the psychic potential in us all. Since psychic
ability is a manifestation of the intuitive faculty, and intuition
is in itself an aspect of mind function, we need to devote at
least one chapter to the mysteries contained within the mind.

YOGA MASTERS ON MIND

Thousands of years before any modern writings on the function of the mind, the yoga masters known as the Rishis existed,

reputedly dwelling in seclusion in the forests of India. Their findings about the human psyche formed the basis for later eastern philosophical teachings, which were passed down orally at first from student to student, and were later written down in the ancient Brahmin texts.

Since the late nineteenth century these teachings have been brought to the West by yogis such as Swami Vivekananda, who was the leading disciple of the great Hindu saint, Sri Ramakrishna. Swami Vivekananda's mission was to bring this ancient wisdom to the West, which he did very success-fully, lecturing extensively in America and Britain. Many of his brilliant lectures are available in published form, and I certainly recommend them to those who wish to learn about the tremendous potential within us all. Perhaps his most out-standing work was entitled *Raja Yoga*,[1] in which he comments on the Aphorisms of Patanjali who was widely regarded as the father of Raja Yoga—the Yoga of control of the mind.

The works of Yogi Ramacharaka were written in the early part of the twentieth century by an Englishman, William Walter Atkinson, in conjunction with Baba Barata who had learnt these teachings in India from Yogi Ramacharaka, his guru. These very readable books throw a beacon of light on the subject of mind potential, among other subjects.

My favourite teacher is the western master of yoga, His Eminence Dr George King. His lectures and writings, which are available through The Aetherius Society, are very simple and clearly explained and, in my view, apply more than' any others I have come across to the modern world in which we live. He has tailored his teachings through his own personal realisation and demonstration, so that they can be safely prac-tised and easily understood by those of us who dwell in the hectic, highly pressured life-styles of the modern era.

One thing all these teachers have in common is that they are not so much theorists, basing their findings on deductions and ideas, as proven practitioners of the psychic sciences in their own right. Each one has entered the deeper states of meditation and has discovered along the way a fund of knowledge available through awakening the faculty of intuition. Experience is, after all, the finest guide to a true understanding of mind potential.

In addition to these yogis, there are many other valuable sources of information about the mind. One thing that all researchers are agreed upon is that we have only scratched the surface in using the full capacity of our mental potential. The mechanism of the human psyche, both on a physical and a metaphysical level, is extraordinarily brilliant, if we only take full advantage of it.

SCIENTIFIC RESEARCH

Spectacular progress has been made in scientific research into the mind, which can add considerably to our understanding. For example, over the last few years researchers have discovered much about the difference between the right- and left-hand sides of the brain. This is a massive subject about which entire treatises have been written, but I shall give a brief summary here of some recent findings.

The two sides of the physical brain are responsible for controlling very different aspects of our mental process. Scientists have discovered that the left-hand side of the brain is concerned with the analytical function of our mind, such as deduction, calculation, memory, logic and all things rational. The right-hand side is concerned with the creative function, such as imagination, visualisation, instinctive realisations and all things intuitive.

Researchers believe that, on the whole, the right-hand function of the brain is neglected in the modern world in favour of the left-hand function, and that there is a serious imbalance as a result of this. Our educational systems have concentrated primarily on deduction and memory and devoted very little time to expanding and developing the creative process. Obviously there are notable exceptions to this, such as the Rudolph Steiner approach to education and others who develop the creative side of our nature within their educational programmes, but certainly the emphasis in most schools has been on calculation, logical expression and remembering a fund of facts, theorems and data. This has also been the content of most examinations which mainly test our memory of data and the ability to present information in a rational way.

But the right-hand side of the brain is equally as important as the left, and this imbalance can be redressed by developing and using the intuitive and creative aspects of our mind. In my opinion it would be a very good thing if a basic course in psychic development was included in educational programmes in schools. Controversial as this may sound, it would have very practical applications, not only in the personal life of children and students, but in their professional life as well.

Many business decisions have to be made partly on the basis of instinct and gut feeling. Those who work in the money markets, for example, would agree with this. Despite the knowledge of economists and bankers around the world, the same information and statistics, when analysed by different experts, produce opposing opinions about where exactly the market will go, the future value of different currencies and so forth. Knowledge and deduction alone, which are attributes associated with the left-hand side of the brain, are not enough to make conclusive decisions.

I am certainly not suggesting that we should try to use our intuitive faculty to make money, although many business people have used methods of divination to assist them in their enterprises, and still do. I have found that if one's motive is purely selfish, intuitive attributes are very limited in their effectiveness. They are far more conducive to unselfish, humanitarian activities. Nevertheless, our obsession with using the left-hand side of the brain far more than the right-hand side is a major limitation, even in the business world.

Other areas of scientific research into the brain over recent years have also drawn some very significant conclusions. One particular series of experiments involved registering the responses of the brain. Before we take any physical action, the brain has transmitted a mental impulse through our nervous system to cause us to walk, lift our hand, scratch or whatever the action may be. The experiments were designed to measure these internal impulses and nervous responses to a fraction of a second, using carefully devised apparatus connected to the people taking part. It was discovered that, in certain cases, the apparatus registered a reaction from the individuals before the brain itself was activated. This reaction took place only a fraction of a millisecond before, but it illustrated something very significant—that thought impulse within a human being does not necessarily originate in the brain but in another part of the human psyche.

Some took this experiment to confirm the existence of the soul and others referred to the existence of 'will' as distinct from the brain. However you interpret it, it does back up what metaphysicians have said for thousands of years: that although the physical brain is very important indeed, it is not the fount of all knowledge. It is not the source of all mind.

THE METAPHYSICAL APPROACH

The word 'metaphysical' literally means that which is beyond the physical. When examining the mind, the metaphysician does not see it as being contained within the physical brain. He sees mind as energy, bringing a close interaction between thought and feeling. For example, inspiration may originate from a feeling, and then be translated into a thought process which manifests itself in literature, science or the arts. The initial seed of the idea or impulse which actually produced that inspired mental process may have been a combination of impressions which are more related to feeling than thought. These feelings cannot be said to have originated in the physical brain, although the physical brain will have translated them into some form of intelligence.

It is interesting to examine the states of being which produce inspiration. The poet Wordsworth describes in some of his poems the virtual state of grace in which a certain oneness with Nature is felt, a state he obviously experienced himself. Religious writings also refer to elevated states of grace or higher consciousness. From a psychic point of view, these states are created when the vibrations within the aura of the person in question have been raised to a high level or frequency. In such a state of consciousness, great inspiration will come to the person in one form or another. It might be poetry; it might be hearing wonderful sounds in one's imagination, which culminate in a great musical work. It might be an inspired realisation which can lead to the invention of an important scientific innovation. It might be a state which leads to a mediumistic rapport with an advanced person who is no longer living in a physical body but now inhabits a higher plane of existence and who gives a message of wisdom and healing. It might be the moment in which a painter sees the interplay of colour in a landscape in a new way and is able to visualise this to such an extent that it can be expressed in a historic work of art. These inspirations result from an elevated state of consciousness, which causes the physical brain to produce great thoughts. The brain is virtually a translating mechanism which helps to express the state of being of the individual.

There is still considerable investigation going on into the exact internal functions that ensue when the brain, for example, causes us to walk or to make any physical movement. Exactly what mental impulses have been sent and how the nervous system responds to those impulses to bring about the action is not fully known. Nor is it known at what stage the subconscious mind becomes involved in this process. These issues are the source of continuing programmes of enquiry and research. From the point of view of this book, it is sufficient to note that although the physical brain is a wonderful mechanism, and a source of fascination and mystery even to those who make it their lifetime study, it is not the sole key to understanding the function of mind.

It is easy to see how western culture has misunderstood the exact nature of enlightenment. Even in the eighteenth century, which is referred to by historians as the Age of Enlightenment in Europe, it was seen almost entirely as a product of the left-hand side of the brain. Deductive logic and reason were the hallmarks of this age. The metaphysician believes that enlightenment is not any single thought, realisation or even discovery. It is a state of being or consciousness in which thoughts, discoveries and so on can be expressed. It involves the left-hand side of the brain, the right-hand side of the brain and more than that, because it also involves the feelings, which are crucial in all forms of psychic development.

THE AURA AND PSYCHIC CENTRES

For all mysticism, occultism and yogic philosophy, the starting point when examining the mind is the aura. This is seen as the source of all mental and emotional functions within the individual. The aura contains a multitude of different energies of a psychic nature, which, as one develops psychically, one can begin to see clairvoyantly. These energies are received through the psychic centres and travel throughout the aura in an intermingling network of psychic channels which were known in Hindu scripts as the *nadis*. In fact the early scripts, known as the *Upanishads*, stated that there are seventy-two thousand of these *nadis* running throughout the aura in a complex matrix of interconnecting channels which produce a balanced flow of energies in the aura, providing we perform certain simple, purifying exercises. Especially recommended for this purpose was the practice of *Pranayama*, the science of correct breathing.

Among the many psychic centres in the aura, there are seven major ones: base of the spine (*muladhara*), sex (*svad-histhana*), solar plexus (*manipura*), heart (*anahata*), throat (*vishudda*), the Christ centre or third eye, positioned where the eyebrows meet (*ajna*), and the Crown centre, positioned just above the head (*sahasrara*). I have included the Sanskrit names in brackets for each of these centres (or *chakras*, as they were known) because so many writings on this subject refer to them under these names. These centres are in the aura and not in the physical body. They are a few inches in front of the body, depending on the individual, and not necessarily positioned exactly opposite the respective physical organ—the heart centre, for example, is in the centre and not the left-hand side. Books abound on this subject, but the illustrations on pp. 23 and 24 give you an idea of the human aura and the location of the seven major psychic centres.

These psychic centres have a practical effect on our daily and nightly lives, whether or not we are aware of their function. The constant interchange of energies which takes place among the psychic centres and interconnecting channels within the aura directly affects our psychic development. Any blockages in this flow of psychic energy will tend to block our psychic perception. Any blockage in the reception or discharge of energies into and out of the aura will also tend to prevent the free flow of intuitive thought.

It is not necessary to have a detailed understanding of just how these psychic centres function and it is probable that very few of those who have written about this subject fully understand it themselves. It is believed by some mystics that those who really know about this do not share their knowledge with others too freely because the information, if misused, accidentally or on purpose, could be extremely damaging.

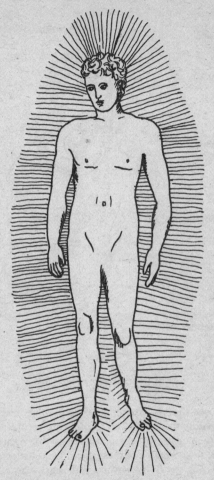

The human aura

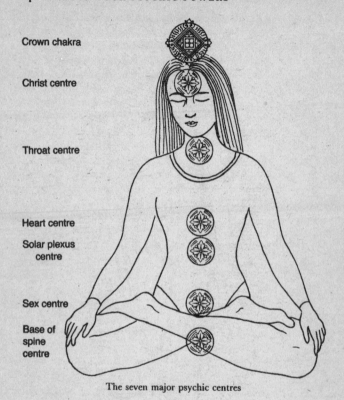

Crown chakra

Christ centre

Throat centre

Heart centre

Solar plexus
centre

Sex centre

Base of
spine
centre

The seven major psychic centres

Those books that do attempt to describe this interchange of energies within the *chakras* and the *nadis* are very often in coded form for the purpose of secrecy which was common in ancient texts. The most notable of these is probably the classic occult treatise *The Serpent Power*, written in the early part of the twentieth century by Sir John Woodroffe,[2] which was based on a hitherto untranslated Sanskrit text. It is a highly complex and somewhat technical but highly informative work for those who can decipher its inner meanings.

In addition to the internal transfer of energies, there is a psychic relationship with the outside environment in which we live. The reason we feel very uplifted in certain country locations is not just the beauty of the scenery and the fresh smell in the air, but also the free-flowing natural energies, or *pranas* as they are termed in Sanskrit, which can rejuvenate our whole being by charging up the psychic centres in our aura. We may not be consciously aware of this process going on, but we will still feel the natural elation caused by it. On the other hand, a ride on an underground train in London or some other busy metropolis is not only stuffy, dirty and imbued with unpleasant noises and smells, but there is also an interaction of energies going on between the passengers, many of whom may be frustrated, tired, irritated or just looking forward to getting off the train. This interchange takes place within the psychic centres and channels within the aura and tends to bring as a result a depleted state of mood and feeling.

If you are in the company of a very dynamic and vibrant person, even if you do not speak to each other, you will start to feel uplifted by his or her presence. If you are in the company of a depressed and pessimistic person, and again nothing is said, almost immediately you may start to feel negative and melancholy yourself. This is a result of the interchange of psychic energies and illustrates the vital importance of this process to our general well-being, as well as our overall psychic development.

Great scientific discoveries and inventions which have taken place while the scientist was in a state of elation, and great works of art which have been produced while the artist was in a highly uplifted state of being, were caused by a positive interaction of psychic energy. This energy, which was attracted to them by the vibration of their aura, affected their psychic centres. Each of these psychic centres controls different aspects of mind and produces an intelligent thought process, which in an exceptional case would be termed genius.

In ancient writings there is usually a tendency to concentrate very heavily on the higher psychic centres, particularly the Christ centre ('third eye') and the Crown centre ('*Brahma Chakra*'). Sometimes an implication runs through these ancient writings that the lower centres should almost be regarded as evils to be avoided as much as possible. More recent writings do not advocate this type of exclusivity of emphasising only the higher centres. A more balanced attitude is generally found nowadays, which is very important to the developing psychic who should strive to use all his psychic attributes in a positive, but always controlled, fashion.

All the psychic centres have a vital function to perform. In certain ways this concentration upon the higher centres in traditional writings is understandable. Material things, which are so valued today, are said to be governed by the lower centres, and sex probably dominates modern cultures as much as it did in imperial Rome and some of the other eras in man's history which can only be regarded as decadent. Advertising, pop music, magazines and youth culture are becoming increasingly obsessed with erotic images, as though the greatest pleasures on earth are found through activating the sex centre. But the elated states brought on by higher centres, activated in the correct manner, can bring greater states of ecstasy and, according to advanced exponents of mysticism, it is only when the Christ centre and ultimately the Crown centre are activated that true, lasting bliss can be experienced.

We should neither reject the lower centres nor ignore the importance of the higher centres, which will give us access to psychic ability and intuition, the more we use them in a careful, balanced manner. When we start to see mind as an interaction of energies creating a thought process through our psychic centres in the aura, we shall have a much clearer idea of how to enhance our psychic awareness.

It is interesting to note that research into the minutiae of atomic particles has shown that the mind of the physicist performing the experiments has, according to some, had a direct effect upon the results. This is one of the reasons why certain physicists are rejecting traditional definitions of proof as being an event which is repeatable under identical physical conditions. They are starting to realise that mind is beyond the purely physical environment and can actually affect the physical outcome of their experiments. Mind over matter, which was hotly disputed by physicists at one time as an impossibility, is now accepted in some form by an increasing number of modern scientists.

For many of us, academic proof of the power of mind over matter is not necessary. Our common sense tells us, for example, that if we are sick and being visited by friends or relatives, certain people will cheer us up far more than others. This is not necessarily because we like them more than others, nor because of their conversation, which may be the last thing we feel like at such a time. But there are certain people who radiate a vibration, before any words are uttered, which is at once uplifting and healing. These vibrations are psychic energies channelled through the psychic centres of the visitor outwards and received by us into our own aura. This process can cause us to feel better, and is in fact a natural form of healing.

THE THREE ASPECTS OF MIND

Mind is generally broken down into three categories: subconscious, conscious and superconscious. There is an abundance of information on these and I particularly recommend the Personal Development cassettes of His Eminence Dr George King on this subject.[3] It is advisable, incidentally, to avoid studying a multitude of different schools of thought on the same subject at the same time. Even though they may all provide very useful information, very often they have different terms of reference and different ways of looking at the same thing, which can be bewildering if studied simultaneously. The word 'subconscious' may mean one thing to a particular teacher, and to another teacher something rather different. I have met extremely well-versed students who found themselves confused by attempting to draw on too many different sources of information on one subject at the same time.

The subconscious mind is the storehouse of memory and instinct. It contains a vast amount of information appertaining to our physical functions, without which we simply could not exist. Psychiatry is being questioned now more than ever and some feel that it has undermined our appreciation of this extraordinary aspect of mind by virtually holding it responsible for a whole variety of innate, vague promptings. Undoubtedly some of these are subconscious, but some are the result of uncontrolled imaginative wanderings which are an uncontrolled use of the creative faculty of our mind. If we were to believe that all the psychological imbalances within us are caused by a warped subconscious mind which, according to some psychiatrists, is usually the result of an unfortunate childhood, we would undervalue the brilliance of this aspect of our being. The subconscious is basically a storehouse for mind energy which we have attracted to ourselves and if we use it correctly it is a wonderful, in-built natural attribute within us all. It is not some frightful skeleton in the cupboard which houses our guilt, fears and all things negative. These things will only be lodged in our subconscious if we have wrongly conditioned it in the past.

The conscious mind is the mental process with which we are most familiar. It is the rational, deductive, intellectual part of our mind which formulates our normal day-to-day thought processes. This also impresses us with our desires and all conscious thoughts.

The most misunderstood and yet most elevated aspect of mind is the superconscious. It is to this aspect we must turn when we are looking to our psychic and spiritual development. The journey from consciousness to superconsciousness, according to metaphysics, is the most important journey any of us can make.

WATCHFULNESS AND VISUALISATION

Certain Buddhist schools refer to the process of watchfulness as one of the simplest ways of contacting the higher aspects of our mind. By watchfulness is meant the process of becoming aware of the function of the conscious mind. It is the procedure through which you can observe the thoughts that enter the consciousness without becoming attached to or involved in them. In order to do this, ideally conditions should be as peaceful and undisturbed as possible. You should be seated comfortably with the back straight or, if you are familiar with them, in one of the recommended yogic postures (asanas). Some would advocate lying down to perform this practice, but I would not recommend that since it can tend to cause drowsiness and even sleep, which is the exact opposite state from the one you are seeking. Watchfulness, as its name would suggest, is an alert and active state. Although you are peaceful and should be as physically relaxed and as still as possible, you should remain mentally active.

You then start to observe your thoughts as they come and go like waves of energy, which in fact they are. Gradually this wave motion of conscious thought will become more and more even, and it is then that you start to gain control over your state of mind. This very simple yet extremely beneficial practice is sometimes called meditation. Meditation to one person is a very different thing from meditation to another. True meditation in its highest sense is an extremely elevated state, far removed from watchfulness, but this is a very good preliminary exercise to perform before going into other practices such as visualisations, which are specifically designed to enhance your psychic development.

You may find it difficult to sustain your mental alertness in this state of watchfulness, especially initially, and it will be necessary, after a period of preparatory unwinding, to introduce a focus for your concentration in the form of a suitable visualisation. Again, visualisations are sometimes described as meditations, depending on your terms of reference. They may well lead to meditation and they provide one of the keys to enhancing your psychic awareness, but they are not true meditation in its most advanced form.

In visualisation we are starting to use the creative aspect of our mind, which scientists would say is governed by the right-hand side of the brain. It is very important in doing this that we avoid any blankness of the mind, always remaining alert. Some teachers go to great lengths to ensure that their students remain alert, even advocating that they stay awake at all times by pinching themselves or using some other more abrasive and painful method. This should not be necessary providing you approach these practices in a determined and dynamic manner.

As you start to observe your mental process through watchfulness, you may encounter some very revealing insights into yourself. The first time we start to see exactly what thoughts are going through our minds is not always pleasant. But rest assured that when this happens to you, you really are starting to make some progress, and it is by remaining balanced, calm and still, virtually an observer, that you will find the key to success in gaining control over your conscious mind. You can then introduce visualisations to help you to cultivate an awareness of your own latent ESP.

2
ESP

*

The whole phenomenon of ESP (extra-sensory perception) has been covered in a veil of mystery for far too long. This has been done mainly by those who have regarded ESP as the preserve of the few who claim to have 'the gift'. Exponents of ESP have tended to see it as their unique, God-given ability, and have encouraged others to leave the whole phenomenon well alone. This type of attitude has fostered an atmosphere of secrecy among psychic practitioners from a whole variety of different historical and geographical cultures.

Even today some people warn against 'dabbling' in anything of a psychic nature. The word 'occult' is bandied around by those who are opposed to the psychic sciences, as though it was a word which denoted evil and wickedness. In fact, the word 'occult' is derived from the Latin and means, literally, 'something hidden, or secret'. Practitioners of the 'black' arts who have described themselves as occultists have provided a convenient label for those who are opposed to all things psychic. Occultists are all too often tarred with the same brush, regardless of their ethical background, when in fact they consist primarily of people who seek in one way or another to discover the hidden or secret sciences connected with the psychic faculty of man.

'Unnatural', 'dangerous' and other similar pejoratives are used by some people when referring to the development of ESP. In fact, nothing could be further from the truth. It is the most natural thing in the world for us to develop and use our extra-sensory faculties, and it is not dangerous providing you follow the careful guidelines which I shall describe in this book.

When the myths and superstitions are stripped away, and when we are no longer fearful of the subject, we can start to see just how helpful the study of ESP really is, for it can greatly enhance our lives provided we make the effort to understand exactly what we are dealing with, and avoid the pitfalls along the way. I shall highlight the most obvious and common of these pitfalls. If you are practical and never lose touch with your inherent common sense, you will find this a most exciting and rewarding journey of discovery into your own latent psychic ability.

PROOF OF ESP

The study of this subject is usually described in academic circles as parapsychology, and it is now being taken more seriously than ever before. Many universities and other academic establishments now regard this as an important area of study, to be considered alongside other more conventional disciplines. This is certainly a welcome development, but it is often regarded by psychics as a limited one, because many academic establishments attempt to apply to parapsychology the same laws devised for the study of the physical sciences. Most psychics believe that it will be necessary fundamentally to re-evaluate the ground rules of traditional study in order to tackle successfully the phenomenon of ESP.

Psychics say that the laws designed for physics cannot be applied to psychic awareness, because ESP is an attribute that is primarily related to individual feeling. They therefore regard some of the scrupulously devised academic experiments performed under laboratory conditions as fundamentally flawed. All too often the scientists concerned have not taken into account how the conditions applied to the experiment affect the feelings of the psychic practitioner upon whom the experiment is being conducted. Inevitably this leads to rather limited and, in some cases, deceptive findings. There is no doubt that many of the researchers are sincere and open-minded in their pursuit of the truth about ESP. But most psychics would argue that they must extend the parameters of their investigative procedures to include such things as moods, the time of day or night, the emotional state of the psychic and other factors which are somewhat foreign to normal laboratory experimentation in an academic environment.

Both Eastern and Western schools of mysticism are united on one point—that the answer to all questions of psychic development can only ultimately be found within the individual. They agree that while outside sources can advise and teach, the final answers can only come from inner experience. They make it clear that, no matter how much physical proof you offer to a sceptical nonbeliever, that person will always find a reason to continue his disbelief if he chooses.

For this reason a tradition has always existed among some practitioners that they should never use displays of ESP to prove their psychic powers. They feel that this is a futile exercise and one which will not bring about the desired result of encouraging others to turn within to their own latent natural abilities. Unfortunately they have tended to keep their knowledge so well hidden that only tested students, who have proved themselves to be of pure heart and mind and capable of the strictest discipline, have been given an initiation into any of these secrets. Many ancient texts now available in bookshops were written in a somewhat coded form, and it often requires some specialised knowledge to understand them.

There are those who make every effort to debunk the concept of ESP at every available opportunity. The most common explanation such people use, when all others fail them, is to label psychic occurrences as mere coincidence. The validity of this argument starts to wane the more familiar you become with ESP. As I shall attempt to show in this book, the existence of ESP tends to point to the exact opposite conclusion— that there really is no such thing as coincidence at all.

Some of the debunking explanations put forward by sceptics may themselves border on the absurd. But more profitable than intellectual debate is personal experience, and I shall leave you to judge whether ESP is a lot of hocus-pocus or whether there really is something in it.

The majority of people today are, at the very least, fascinated by this whole subject, even though they probably do not fully understand it. I have met very few who do not have a story to tell from their own lives, which points to the existence of some form of ESP. I am sure that you can think back to some incident in your own life or the life of a close friend or relative, which cannot be explained away by pure physics as we know it. ESP leaves the realm of physics and commences a fascinating journey into the realm of metaphysics. In taking this journey, it is advisable to keep your feet firmly on the ground, always acknowledging the vital importance of a balanced approach to the physical world, as you start to look beyond this into something higher.

IMPRESSIONS

We form all kinds of impressions—in fact it is amazing just how instantaneously we do form them. Sometimes an impression can be formed about a happening before it even takes place. You yourself may have said, when talking about a forthcoming event, 'I've got a good feeling about this.' This type of statement is frequently made, often when there really is not sufficient information to make a rational comment about the happening in question. The psychologist will claim that these feelings are purely subconscious, aroused by deeply-buried memories. Maybe this is sometimes the case, but it certainly cannot be applied to all cases.

For example, the detective's famous hunch can often be more reliable than the deductive process, because it is not limited solely to available information. It cannot be a purely subconscious reaction because the detective may not have a fund of memory to call on which applies to a specific case in hand. It is not a deductive process, nor purely a subconscious reaction: there must be some other aspect of mind being trapped when the detective gets his hunch.

Psychologists see impressions as instinctive reactions, usually based upon the suppressed likes and dislikes of the individual concerned. Occasionally this may be true, but certainly not always. For example, an impression of foreboding can be experienced, which goes against our wishes in a particular case. We may find a person or situation very attractive and very desirable, but nevertheless we experience this feeling of foreboding. The acid test rests on whether the feeling of foreboding proves to be accurate. If it does, we must learn to listen to our feelings. If our impressions become reliable in many differing situations in life, they must be seen to represent an intuitive attribute and not a purely subconscious one.

These impressions, hunches and vibrations all go to indicate that there is an entirely different process at work in our mental faculty than either conscious deduction or subconscious prompting. Often this mysterious faculty is referred to as intuition. It is certainly a form of mental faculty, but it is one that is connected to our feelings as well as our thoughts.

I have always found that the most profitable way to study ESP is not so much to look at the many thousands of cases and claims which other people make, but rather to examine your own life. Other people's examples can be regarded with suspicion, or at least uncertainty, but personal experience is something we can all rely on. Others may question your own experiences, but you know whether they happened or not. It is difficult sometimes to prevent the doubts of others from convincing you that your own experience did not really happen or that you misunderstood it at the time.

COMMON EXAMPLES OF ESP

Some common occurrences may be fairly banal and yet, if examined carefully, rather interesting. For example, have you ever thought about a person and, at that very instant, he walked into the room, or telephoned you, or rang the front door bell? If you have, did you have a good reason to expect him to do this, or was it most unlikely? If it happened at the exact instant that you thought of him, and you had no reason to expect him to do so at that time, it must surely be regarded as an interesting turn of events, to say the least. After all, it could not be the result of conscious deduction, because you had no reason to deduce that he would contact you at that time. Nor could it be a result of any subconscious response within you, because, since no prior arrangement had been made with this other person, directly or indirectly, there was no expectation lodged in your memory.

Such a simple and admittedly mundane case as this leaves us, as far as I can see, with only two possible explanations. Either it was an example of the intuitive faculty at work, or it was a pure coincidence. Paradoxically, the theory of coincidence to explain these extremely common occurrences is used frequently by orthodox scientific thinkers who, in their own line of work, would not be satisfied with such an explanation: they would seek a more logical one. To be fair, we might allow the sceptic a certain number of coincidences, even though personally I do not believe in coincidence at all. But when events like this happen over and over again—and there are very few people who cannot recount some form of ESP experience in their lives—then we have to look elsewhere for an explanation. It just does not stand up to basic common sense to maintain that all the multitude of ESP cases throughout history, some clothed in a religious context and some not, were just examples of coincidence. That theory gets a very hollow ring to it after a while.

Everyday examples of ESP can be given by the score. Why do you feel you should visit a particular shop on a particular day for no apparent reason, and then meet someone there whom you have been wanting to meet? You are pressed into going to a jumble sale which you would not normally go to, and yet you find there the very book you have been searching for in bookshops and libraries for months. Examples like this happen to people all over the world all the time. Most of us do not bother even to analyse them when they happen: we just regard them as fortunate or remarkable events.

It would be instructive sometimes to think for a moment. Why did you go to that shop or that jumble sale? Such an analysis of impressions and feelings is unfamiliar to us. We are not taught to do this in schools, where the emphasis is upon training our memories and learning to analyse things rationally. Academic study usually confines the training of memory to facts and figures rather than feelings and inner experiences. We are also taught to use our logical faculty to argue, calculate and deduce. But although these mental processes are stressed in our educational systems, the intuitive faculty is usually neglected and therefore undeveloped in most people, unless they have shown an inherent ability in that direction almost from birth.

If we applied ourselves to analysing our intuition more often, we would start to get some very interesting results. What exactly caused us to walk down a particular road instead of the one we normally take, as a consequence of which we met a particular person who invited us to attend a particular function at which we met the person we later married? Was it all totally haphazard? Did we get a prompting to walk down that particular road instead of the one we normally take? Did we get any special feeling or impression at that time? Such an analysis might lead us to the view that there is an inherent, untapped aspect of mind that is latent within us all. It could also lead us to the conclusion that life is not as haphazard as it appears to be, and that there is in fact a specific design or destiny factor behind the events and occurrences we all experience.

One of the best starting points from which to develop our own ESP is to study the principles that lie behind the intriguing science of divination.

3
The Science of Divination

*

Most popular newspapers regard it as essential nowadays to include in their pages an astrological column where readers can study their 'stars' for the day. Some readers see this simply as a light-hearted diversion, but others take it far more seriously. Thousands of people make it a daily habit to study their 'stars', to see what the day holds in store for them. This trend is not restricted to the publishing world of newspapers and magazines, but is often found on radio and television as well.

This preoccupation with divination is certainly not new. Civilisations throughout the ages have always included, in one form or another, seers, oracles and prophets. The twentieth century is no exception in showing this consistent inclination in mankind to believe in some form of prediction. Despite the proliferation of atheistic philosophies and political creeds in modern times, the fascination with divination in one form or another has not waned. In fact, according to some media reports, the interest among people from all walks of life and different educational and social backgrounds is on the increase.

NOSTRADAMUS

The word 'divination' is derived from 'divine', and literally means using one's divine nature. One of the most commonly held associations with divination is that of prophecy, and one immediately thinks of such famous historical figures as Nostradamus. It is not clear whether Nostradamus used a form of clairaudience or clairvoyance to practise his prophecy, since he was very careful to wrap up in secrecy everything about his method and even the substance of the prophecies themselves. His texts have had a multitude of different interpretations and meanings attributed to them since they were composed in the sixteenth century, but they have remained a constant source of fascination and many intriguing attempts have been made to understand them.

Nostradamus' prophecies consist of six hundred texts, or quatrains as they are called, with very obscure references, few of which can be readily understood. Their very obscurity means that they cannot really provide any practical or useful information for the reader. They have been used frequently, though, to prove the validity of prophecy, and enthusiastic Nostradamus disciples have helped to justify this claim.

The unsatisfactory aspect of Nostradamus' work is that so much of it remains inconclusive. It does not serve the purpose of teaching, advising, warning or even trying to change the course of events. It does, however, provide a very useful source of information for the serious student and has satisfied many people that there is such a thing as prophecy. Because it was so dangerous politically and regarded by the religious establishments of the day as heretical to practise prophecy—never mind the other occult practices Nostradamus was reputed to perform—it was probably in the interests of caution that the wording was so wrapped up in secrecy and code.

In some ways the demonstration of prophecy by Nostradamus has much in common with demonstrations by yoga practitioners and occultists to prove their psychic or magical abilities to sceptics. These attempts are nearly always unsuccessful, in that the hardened sceptic will usually find some reason to debunk them. Even today, in a far more liberal age, we still see self-styled paranormal investigators setting out to disprove psychic abilities in one way or another. One of their favourite methods is to show that these psychic demonstrations could easily be performed through straightforward conjuring. Of course their logic is flawed, because even if a conjuror were capable of duplicating some of these feats, it would not in any way prove that they were not psychic in nature when performed by the occultist or yogi. It does, however, illustrate a point made through the ages—that it is not worth trying to prove your psychic powers to disbelievers. When they are ready they will discover these things for themselves.

DIVINATION AND RELIGION

Divination involves, to some degree, using the superconscious mind which is that aspect of mind nearest to our true divine nature. It is strange that although psychic practices have been linked to religions throughout history, so often orthodox branches of them try to condemn and prevent psychic development. If you decide to take to the path of psychic development you may well encounter opposition and it is best to be forewarned about this. There is nothing unchristian about developing and using psychic abilities, providing you use them only to serve and help others. There are sections of St Paul's letters, as published in the New Testament, which can be construed to mean that he encouraged the development of psychic abilities. This is one interpretation, for example, of Corinthians Book 1, Chapter 14. Far be it from me, however, to enter a theological debate based on biblical interpretation, since one thing that historical research has proved beyond any doubt is that the literal accuracy of the Bible is highly questionable.

I do not bring this up to denigrate any religious faith or teaching, but to give confidence to the developing psychic not to be discouraged by any form of religious bigotry. I am sure that many readers of this book will be regular churchgoers, which is completely compatible with psychic development. This can go hand in hand with religious worship, including Christianity or any other spiritual doctrine. It is interesting to note just how many types of psychic experience described by many different religions and cultures transcend all barriers of orthodox dogma. The similarities between so-called miracles and psychic happenings across the religious barriers of Hinduism, Judaism, the Islamic faith, Buddhism and Christianity in fact prove the essential oneness of all religious teaching.

You may well not regard yourself as religious at all, but that, too, should not prevent you from developing your own inner potential.

DIFFERING APPROACHES TO DIVINATION

The first thing you find when examining the various schools of divination, and the multitude of practitioners professing their skills, is that there is no single organisation or body overseeing them all, although there are several groups and organisations to which practitioners can belong. Because of this I would advocate a cautious approach when first investigating practitioners of divination. It is the easiest thing in the world to set yourself up as a practitioner in any one of a variety of forms of divination.

Nor is there any need for a practitioner to produce any form of qualification, although a number of organisations in the various disciplines do run thorough training courses which result in some form of qualification. There are also excellent practitioners who have no recognised qualification at all, but get accurate results.

One cannot be too careful in examining the whole area of divination, precisely because it is so effective and revealing when practised correctly. If it were not there would be no need for cautious discrimination—it could justifiably be dismissed as trivial nonsense. Having myself practised the psychic sciences for many years and discussed these concerns with a wide variety of fellow practitioners, I would recommend the following useful yardsticks to help you discriminate between exponents of the science of divination.

Be wary of anybody who claims to be able to tell you your fortune. This may sound very surprising to you, since divination is often thought of as a form of fortune-telling. A deeper examination of the concept of prediction, however, shows that there is a vast difference between helping people to make the most of their lives through an understanding of their potential destiny and telling them their fortune. This difference is absolutely critical to understanding divination.

There is a very important dividing line between a belief in unalterable predestination and a belief in a person's possible destiny, dependent on how fully he or she lives up to it. Predestination is a fatalistic concept which usually implies a belief in a superior force or fate that has completely mapped out our lives. According to this view, no matter what we may do, nothing can alter our predetermined fate. But the whole value of divination is based on and derives from exactly the opposite principle. The diviner recognises that there is a destiny pattern in all our lives: through a careful and balanced reading of this pattern, certain areas of weakness can either be avoided or overcome, and certain areas of strength can be fully capitalised upon, expanded and used to the best possible advantage.

Exponents of divination often believe that this destiny pattern operates in cycles or rhythms. Practitioners from a variety of schools of thought and methods agree that, as well as certain overall destiny features which affect the whole life of a person, there are certain specific times in that life which are auspicious for some things and not for others. Far from telling a person her fortune as though it were cast in stone, the science of divination identifies these life trends and cycles with the express purpose of enabling the individual to live his or her life more successfully and with greater fulfilment.

To know one's predetermined future without being able to avoid certain pitfalls or enhance certain positive attributes would relegate one to the position of an automaton. There would then be no element of the unexpected or of individual achievement. Under these conditions it would arguably be better not to know one's future.

The person who seeks a reading, whom I will refer to as 'the subject', often wishes to know exactly what will happen to her and will try to encourage practitioners to commit themselves to various dogmatic predictions. Very few exponents of these sciences, who really understand their chosen method, will succumb to this kind of pressure. They know that it will not be in the long-term interests of their subject to imply any kind of fatalism or predestination, although they should be able to predict some definite trends in that person's life.

It is tempting for exponents of the science of divination to make it sound much easier than it really is for the subject to overcome the difficulties in her life. There is a natural tendency to dwell far more on the positive aspects of what they see than on the negative ones. This has the added advantage of making the reading more popular, in the short term at least, and if they are disposed to make money from this practice, it can appear much more lucrative to do just this. The end result, though, will not be an honest and truly helpful reading.

Divination's most valuable contribution to all of us is to identify those lessons we were born to learn. Of course, these vary from person to person and that is why the individual reading can be so helpful and advantageous if it is given along the right lines. A good exponent of these sciences will know how to identify the lessons of an individual, or the major ones at least, and will also be able to give some pointers as to how the best possible advantage can be gleaned from them. He or she will certainly not advise the subject to ignore these lessons, but will give advice on how and possibly when to deal with the issues as they arise, and so become the better for them. It would make life fairly pointless if there were no lessons or experiences to be gained, and the most worthwhile aspect of a good reading is the greater degree of control we can gain over the experiences of life and the consequent understanding this brings.

A practitioner will identify your good qualities and, if he is honest, those areas where character development may be required or where the expression of certain latent abilities is as yet dormant or only partially manifested. Again, there is the temptation for a reader greatly to overemphasise the positive aspects in relation to the negative ones, in view of the obvious popularity of such an approach. A highly complimentary reading may also seem to be a marvellously revealing one to those who seek to be flattered.

Those areas where character development is necessary are part of the challenge of life and, some would say, the most rewarding part. A good practitioner would therefore attempt to identify these and give strong pointers as to how best to deal with them. Of course, this is a highly sensitive area and, unless he is properly qualified, the practitioner should not attempt to trespass upon the zone of psychotherapy but stick strictly within his brief, namely the divination of potential aspects of the subject's life. As well as divining the future potential of individuals, organisations and even countries, these sciences are also able to reveal much about their characteristics and qualities.

PRACTITIONERS OF DIVINATION

The ability to know one's limits is a key factor in successful divination. The subject who visits the practitioner naturally wants to be told as much as possible, with as much detailed information as possible. Very often the reader will be pressed for precise answers, such as exact dates, locations and names connected with events in the future and so forth. Here the mettle of the reader is severely tested. The practitioner must be able to say, 'I do not know', to such questions, if he does not truly know the answers. In fact, I have found that with few exceptions one must be wary of those practitioners who describe highly detailed and precise, fixed patterns for the future of their subjects. Surprising as it may sound, this is a golden rule in carefully discriminating about the overall credibility of the reader.

This fact should not be used as an excuse by readers for not giving enough information to the subject. But there is a difference between throwing considerable light on a person's potential and giving him or her absolutely definite, specific details as though they were pre-ordained. A good exponent of divination will be able to pinpoint certain key events which may or may not yet have happened in the subject's life, without being told about them. But very rarely do those who are experienced in this science make dogmatic statements about exactly when and how such events will happen.

A reader should not hesitate to suggest possibilities rather than feel the need to make dogmatic predictions, even though many subjects may ask for them. This is really a test of the integrity and honesty of the diviner. The most dangerous reading of all is one in which a lot of precise and detailed information is given, some of which is accurate and some of which turns out to be inaccurate. When the subject sees some of the predictions and statements work out exactly as given, he or she will tend to believe that everything in that reading will turn out to be true. If this is not the case, it may be confusing and misleading to the subject.

Timing in particular is a very variable factor, which depends to a large extent upon the individual concerned. At the time of giving the reading there may be a certain sequence of timing which a reader can pinpoint accurately. Later, the subject may change herself and her life to such an extent that the sequence of timing alters, although the event itself is still relevant to her destiny. The wise exponent of divination will have given the detailed timing information as a potential opportunity rather than a fixed occurrence. The system of divination should reveal certain cycles or periods when specific types of event are likely to occur, but even these are subject to a certain degree of change depending upon the will and life pattern of the individual.

In the final analysis, the reading is intended to be for the help and guidance of the subject—not a demonstration of the prowess of the person giving the reading. Interestingly enough, many exponents of these sciences will say that the more significant the life of the subject, the less easy it is to be dogmatic about minor details in that life. This may be because other major details and influences impinge upon the destiny of such a life path far more than they do upon a comparatively uneventful one. By the same token these major life paths, such as that of the late Sir Winston Churchill, for example, often show a major destiny force at work which in the case of Churchill he was well aware of and commented upon.

All this should not be taken to justify a reader in giving a sparse and uninformative reading. A good practitioner will be able to supply a considerable amount of very useful information, often including possible dates, places and names, to give a fuller idea of the individual's potential life trends. There is no harm at all in such a reader asking questions of the subject, but he will also supply details and information unknown to the subject at that particular time.

The key factor in good divination is really very obvious, but absolutely crucial to the effectiveness of a reader. It could loosely be described as wisdom, understanding and psychological insight. His understanding of life, people and general experience will affect greatly the kind of interpretation he places upon his divining skills.

The choice of whom to visit for a reading is of course up to the subject, who should know something of the background of the practitioner he or she is visiting. This information can either be gained by personal recommendation from others who have made such a visit or from information available about the practitioner. As they say, one's man meat is another man's poison in this respect. However, there are certain specific 'do nots' I would suggest, some of which are fairly obvious but should still be mentioned.

It is not advisable to visit a practitioner who is known to abuse drugs or alcohol or who has been associated with any kind of criminal activity or other overtly immoral behaviour. I would particularly warn against visiting any practitioner of the 'black' arts, and here you have to be a little careful. Usually they will not advertise their leanings, but closer examination of the symbols and other references in their literature or practice may make it clear that they have such connections. Common sense will steer you clear of undesirable practitioners providing you examine carefully whom you are visiting before doing so.

Some people are very opposed to practitioners charging a fee. I would not necessarily agree with this, although I personally choose to donate all the fees I receive towards healing and charitable causes. Providing the practitioner is effective and well-versed and has the necessary attributes, which may have taken him many years to develop, there is no reason why a fee should not be charged. The rate will vary from practitioner to practitioner, and in this field it can certainly be said that the level of the fee, or non-fee as the case may be, is not always an indication of the merit of the practitioner. Providing the fee is not extortionate it is really not an important factor in making a choice of practitioners. It is up to the subject to decide whether or not he or she is willing to pay such a fee.

Experienced practitioners of the science of divination will never use their skills for party games or tricks. They know that it is more than a fairground stunt and that something will be lost to them and the subject if they play at it. There is nothing wrong at all in a practitioner asking a subject for information during the course of a reading. The subject is not there to test him as though it were a contest or game. She is there to seek advice and the practitioner may need certain information to help him give a fuller reading. Many practitioners find it unhelpful to get too much information from the subject before giving a reading, but techniques vary among different readers. A good reader will always prove his ability to the subject in one way or another through the revelation of certain relevant and very valuable information.

It is always worth remembering that you do not go to a practitioner of divination for stimulation, so much as for guidance. Some very good practitioners tend to be rather conservative and go out of their way to avoid making any statements unless they are absolutely sure of them. On the surface this may appear less impressive, but in the long run it is not, because they will never mislead the subject who has visited them. Giving a reading is, after all, a very responsible undertaking, and should not be treated lightly.

ASTROLOGY

Having looked at the differences between practitioners, let's examine some of the systems of divination that are readily available. Of all of them, the most popular and certainly the most famous is astrology. Books on different aspects of this subject abound and are on sale in most major bookshops nowadays. However, for those who are totally unfamiliar with the workings of this science, let me give a very brief and basic description of it.

The philosophy behind astrology is the same as that behind all forms of divination. It hinges on the belief that nothing happens by chance and that by reading the signs of life one can discover a pattern that will reveal much about the destiny of an individual. This pattern is defined by an astrological chart and an expert in this practice can, through interpreting a chart, draw out a fund of useful information and guidance.

The astrologer calculates the exact position of the sun, moon and planets in the solar system, in relation to the place and time of birth of the subject. From this, he can discover information about the life, character and destiny of any individual, group or organisation. The procedures used in determining these positions and their meanings have been developed over thousands of years.

Of course the complete practice of astrology is far more advanced than the daily 'stars' in the newspaper, magazine or other media outlet. These daily 'stars' only refer to the Sun Signs of individuals—in other words the position of the sun relative to their place and time of birth. Hence the entire population of the world is grouped together under only twelve separate headings and all those of the same Sun Sign are given the same reading for the day. This is an extremely approximate form of astrology which is not taken very seriously by experts in this very ancient and fascinating science.

The astrologer will say that no two charts are exactly the same. After all, the position of all planets as well as the sun and moon have to be taken into account, and this produces what might be described as a 'complex matrix of influences', as illustrated in the astrological wheel on the opposite page. It is the interpretation of this matrix which sorts the men from the boys, as it were, and reveals the true skills of the astrologer in question.

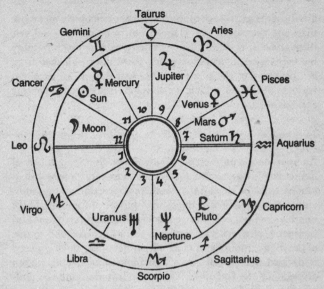

The astrological wheel. A typical chart showing the signs of the zodiac and planets in specific positions

The question of twins is often raised, since they would apparently have identical astrological charts. The expert would point out that even twins have a gap between their moments of birth and this gap may be critical in producing slightly different influences on their destinies. In a case like this, interpretation guided by the intuition is critical, because although twins may have similar characteristics they may have very different destinies, as many examples prove.

This element of intuitive interpretation is absolutely crucial and really makes the difference between just a good astrologer and a great astrologer. Although astrology is a precise science, there are always questions which depend upon the interpretive ability of the astrologer concerned. I have personally met more than one astrologer who claimed not to be psychic and yet, through his or her skill, demonstrated a definite psychic ability by discovering information which could not be gleaned from the positions of the planets alone. Astrology is an excellent springboard from which to develop one's latent psychic abilities.

NUMEROLOGY

Another excellent method of divination is the practice of numerology. Again, this system involves very precise calculations—in this case of the numbers appertaining to an individual or association at the time of birth or inception. These numbers are not only derived from the date of birth, but also the name, of which each letter is taken to correspond to one of the digits from one to nine. The system of calculation used is derived not only from eastern philosophy but also often draws upon the Kaballah. The Kaballistic tradition is a philosophy which has its roots in Jewish mysticism, and some would say even before this, in the teachings of ancient Egypt. As in the case of astrology, many books have been written about the Kaballah and the magical practices associated with it, and to those who have studied it the emphasis upon the power of numbers and letters will be very familiar.

Again, the fundamental principle of numerology is that nothing happens by chance, and therefore the numbers associated with a person at the time of his birth will point towards his destiny. An analysis of these numbers reveals information about his character and, in my view, the intuitive faculty plays an essential part in interpreting these factors. When you consider that people change constantly, some far more than others, throughout their lives, this intuitive faculty is essential to a full assessment of the chart of an individual relative to his or her current position in life. If all life were fixed in some predetermined, unalterable pattern, then the numbers alone might be enough to determine a person's destiny. But it is this element of change, and the fact that we make our own choices within certain overall parameters of destiny, character, will and so on, which really make life worth living. Numerology and astrology form an excellent basis for an individual reader to develop the intuitive promptings of his or her mind, which can respond to this element of change.

THE TAROT

This system follows the principle that the spread of cards of the Tarot pack, which are selected by the subject, are not chosen by chance. Again, the belief that there is no such thing as coincidence lies behind this practice of divination through the interpretation of the seventy-eight Tarot cards. Each card denotes certain characteristics, qualities or forces and the reader can interpret them to reveal likely occurrences in the destiny of the subject. Very few exponents of the Tarot deny the importance of their intuitive faculty in determining what each combination of cards indicates for the subject. The reader must draw upon his or her psychic ability as well as the knowledge of the meaning of each of the cards of the Tarot pack.

Nowadays, some fascinating work is also being conducted by Jungian therapists using the Tarot pack. In particular, they use the twenty-two master cards of the pack, also known as the major arkana, as images to help clients identify with their corresponding archetypes. Although this is not strictly divination, it does go to illustrate how universal some of these systems are becoming and how they can be used to help people in a variety of ways other than their popular association with divination.

THE I CHING

Another very effective system often used for divination is the I Ching or Book of Changes.[1] This is an ancient Chinese system which has its roots in the traditional mystic philosophy of the early Chinese sages, and is based on a book which is available in many bookshops and was regarded at one time as the Bible of the Chinese Adepts.

The practice of the I Ching requires a certain type of intuitive realisation, which is absolutely essential in interpreting this very unusual system of teaching and philosophy. The sage Confucius, who devoted many years to writing profound discourses about this work, stressed the need to become at one with the Book of Changes in order really to understand it. It is also said by practitioners of the I Ching that the book must be approached with a degree of reverence and respect before it can be used successfully for divination purposes.

The use of the I Ching, like the other systems I have briefly described, follows the principle that nothing happens by chance. Yarrow stalks are allowed to fall into an apparently haphazard pattern or, more recently, a system of throwing coins is sometimes used. The fall of the yarrow stalks or the throw of the coins repeated six times results in one of sixty-four combinations known as hexagrams. Each of these, when interpreted, provides an answer to a question which has been posed mentally or in writing before commencing the ritual. Alternatively, it can be practised in a more general way to bring general guidance and advice at a particular time, without a specific question being posed beforehand.

Several books have been written about the I Ching, giving revealing insights into an ancient Chinese philosophy now very much lost in the mists of time. It is generally agreed, though, that it is intuition that provides the key to understanding this ancient system.

OTHER SYSTEMS OF DIVINATION

Chinese astrology is fascinating and sometimes extremely accurate, but it is not used so much for divination purposes for individuals as for revealing their character traits. Each sign in the Chinese Zodiac is associated with the year of birth of the subject and its position in the Chinese calendar. Every year, the dawning of the Chinese New Year is celebrated, heralding one or other of the signs of the Chinese Zodiac, and believers look for the characteristics of that sign to become manifest during the coming year.

Another very famous system which I should at least mention is palmistry. This is derived from the study of the natural lines on the left and right palms of the hand. According to the palmist these have not arrived haphazardly but indicate very definite qualities and destiny features in the life of the subject. Once again the palmist does not believe in chance or coincidence but in a destiny which can change and evolve according to the will and determination of the subject.

Many other systems exist for which there is not enough space in this book, and there must be many which have not even been spoken or written about publicly. But they all require, at least to some degree, the awakening of the psychic forces of the practitioner.

PSYCHIC ABILITY AND DIVINATION

Few practitioners would disagree with the idea that some form of psychic ability is necessary to practise the science of divination. Those who do would claim that these systems are purely scientifically based and that there is no need for an intuitive dimension to interpretation. It can all be analysed, they would say, mathematically or analytically, based only upon the planets, numbers, hand lines, cards, hexagrams or whatever other system they are using to enquire into the future and inner potential of the subject.

Psychics would counter this line of argument by pointing out that the methods used by practitioners are not entirely consistent. Although there is broad agreement on major aspects of all of them, there are also definite areas of difference. In astrology, the existence of certain planets such as Pluto was not known about and therefore not taken into account by early astrologers. Comparatively recent studies have thrown tremendous light upon the influence on astrology of this particular planet, which has added a new dimension to astrological charts. In numerology, the calculation of the length of the cycles into which a lifespan is divided may vary. In the Tarot, a different emphasis has been placed upon certain cards by different experts and the design of the pack can be a critical factor in influencing a particular reading.

The fact that, in spite of these technical changes and differences, the sciences of divination have been successfully practised by practitioners from different schools of thought for many centuries, indicates that calculation is not the only factor at work here. Certainly the practitioner should draw upon all the information at his disposal from his knowledge and technical understanding of the science. This information is extremely important and will play a major role in the effectiveness of the reading. But added to this will be the reader's psychic ability which is enhanced by his or her psychological reaction to the divination process taking place, and this combination of technical and intuitive skills makes for a truly excellent reading.

For example, even though the effect of Pluto was not known about at one time and therefore could not be referred to directly by astrologers, an expert may have been able to draw upon the missing technical information at an intuitive level and still produce a complete and definitive reading for the subject. To summarise, you might say that these systems form an essential deductive basis from which the intuitive abilities of the practitioner can flow.

CHOOSING YOUR SYSTEM

In order to use one of these systems to develop your intuition, as well as to give an effective reading, you need to choose a method that conforms well to your own character and inclination. I would go even farther than this and say that you should try, if possible, to develop a real love for the system of your choice. It is through this love and feeling that you will release the full magical potential of the system and therefore of yourself as the reader.

A highly methodical person, for example, who likes neatness, precision and detailed organisation, might be attracted to a system which uses a method of mathematical calculation. This would apply most obviously to numerology but also, to a very considerable degree, to astrology. An interest in the cosmos and an attraction to all things astronomical would naturally tend to draw one towards astrology. An interest in oriental philosophy, together with perhaps an attraction for Taoism or Confucianism, would draw one towards the I Ching. Those with an interest in magic and the Kaballah are very often drawn to using the Tarot. Incidentally, I would advise against using a Tarot pack which has been devised by an exponent of 'black' magic, no matter how picturesque the design may be, since it can attract negative influences.

Very often an individual will be drawn naturally into the orbit of one or other of these systems, and life itself will virtually bring about a particular vocation or feeling for a specific system. The better the feeling you have for a method of divination, the better it will work for you. In this respect, it has much in common with the practice of the healing arts. For example, those practitioners who are strongly drawn to massage, osteopathy, acupuncture, herbalism or any other system of natural medicine will find that it is likely to work more effectively for them.

If you wish to explore the science of divination, and you

are not drawn to any particular system initially, you would be best advised to study all the various possibilities and see which of them, if any, starts to appeal to you most. If you then decide to pursue it, you will begin to create virtually a personal relationship with it, and through studying it and more importantly practising it, the inner power of divination will start to unfold within you.

As a former music student, I can see strong comparisons between learning the skills of divination and learning to play a piece of music. The piece may seem very difficult at first, and initially all the student's efforts, skill and concentration may have to be applied simply to learning the notes and mastering the techniques required to play it. But once he has mastered the piece technically, he can then lend a portion of his concentration and mental ability to introducing the element of feeling and intensity. Without the technique he will never be able to play the piece of music; but without the feeling and intensity, even if he did play, it would be lifeless and lacking in musical power. It is this feeling and intensity which virtually put flesh upon the bones of the piece of music.

Exactly the same principle applies to the practice of divination. First you need to learn the techniques, knowledge and calculations associated with your chosen system of divination. But later, gradually, you will introduce your higher feelings into this practice, and it is through these feelings that the interpretative skills will be enriched by the element of intuition from within yourself. The process of giving readings will not only help others, but will also start to unfold from within you, the reader, an unrealised inner potential which can open up an exciting new world of personal discovery to you as you start to awaken your faculty of intuition.

4

The Faculty of Intuition

*

There are some systems which rely more upon pure psychic
ability than those already mentioned, and it is to these that
I shall now turn. They are methods which are less organised
and more abstract in nature. They do not require the deductive, analytical approach to the same degree, although, as
in all psychic work, discrimination must always be present.
But they do utilise the faculty of intuition to a very considerable degree in order to be effective.

Probably the most famous of these more abstract methods
is the use of the crystal ball. Despite its renown, comparatively
few words have been written about it. We very often hear
from politicians, industrialists and financiers the old platitude
'I haven't got a crystal ball' when they are discussing future
trends in the world economy. What they mean by this is that
they have no way of knowing exactly what will happen. The
crystal ball, probably more than any other method of divination, is regarded as a symbol of clairvoyance and prophecy.
In fact it can be a very effective instrument for developing the
inherent faculty of intuition that exists within us all.

SCRYING

Unfortunately the crystal ball has been associated with images of fairground readers and gypsy caravans. Undoubtedly some Romanies were, and in certain cases still are, proficient exponents of crystal-gazing. But all too often it is used nowadays as a stunt for entertainment by impostors who want to cash in on the gypsy image.

Some believe that crystal-gazing has its origins in the ancient practice of scrying—the art of divining through looking at reflections. Often mirrors or looking glasses are used, but in fact any substance which reflects an image can be utilised in scrying. Perhaps the first substance to be used was water, and in this context the old saying 'still waters run deep' is highly relevant. A still pool or pond reflects images, and through gazing at these the practitioner awakens his intuitive faculties to perform a reading.

PSYCHOMETRY

The material from which a crystal ball is made has a mystical significance. It is possible that at one time pure crystal was used. If this is so it was an object primarily used for a practice known as psychometry, which is also an extremely effective method for the developing psychic to learn to use. It is the basis of many of the more abstract methods of divination and so it may be helpful if I explain briefly how it works.

Psychometry is the ability to tune in psychically to an object. Through tuning in, the psychometrist learns much about the object, its history and those people who have been connected with it. A psychometrist will take a ring, or other object which has been frequently worn by a subject, hold it in his hands or between his fingers, and tune in to the psychic vibrations contained within this object. These vibrations have been left in the object by the person who has worn it and they will reveal much to the psychometrist about the past thoughts, feelings and actions of the subject. If psychometry is taken far enough, this insight into the past of the subject may lead the psychometrist into divination because psychically he will start to see something of the subject's future. At this point a full reading can be given by the psychometrist who is then tapping into his intuitive faculty on a more abstract level.

Whether you take psychometry this far or not, it is certainly an excellent starting point for psychic development and one that I thoroughly recommend. Some psychometrists apply their skills to antiquarian objects and artefacts in order to learn more about the past history of these objects and through them enhance their knowledge of that period of history. Sometimes they will concentrate on a particular era, such as ancient Egypt or Greece. This can be very effective, but the findings of such psychometry are very difficult to verify since the psychometrist is usually moving into uncharted waters. No historian really knows exactly what happened in these ancient civilisations. Nevertheless it can be a very revealing practice to perform psychometry upon ancient objects.

It is now generally recognised by parapsychologists that the most conducive material for storing psychic vibrations is quartz crystal. Therefore, from a psychometric point of view, it is possible to perform a very powerful reading from an object made of crystal, which has either been worn or associated with an individual or has a particularly interesting history.

THE CRYSTAL BALL

If the crystal ball has its origins in psychometry, it has evolved into an entirely different system which, in some cases, is almost the exact opposite from psychometry, although in both practices the faculty of intuition is absolutely crucial. In most cases, the last thing a crystal-gazer would want to use is a crystal ball which is actually made of pure crystal. Quartz crystal attracts and stores psychic vibrations and impressions which are then very difficult to remove from the crystal. The practice of crystal-gazing, as it has evolved, requires as open and unobstructed an environment as possible to allow the flow of intuition. The psychic vibrations which would be attracted during readings from each subject into a quartz crystal ball would greatly interfere with this open flow of intuition. One would tend to pick up the vibrations of subjects with very magnetic personalities, who have a dynamic presence and have left their mark as it were in the form of vibrations channelled into the crystal ball during previous readings. These vibrations could well interfere with other subjects who come in the future and could cause considerable confusion.

Apart from these psychic reasons against using quartz crystal, the cost of a pure crystal ball would be immense and completely impractical for most people.

For these reasons, crystal balls are made nowadays from crystal glass. They vary considerably in size and can be anything from two inches in diameter to seven inches in diameter or more. Some people recommend the smaller type of crystal which can be picked up and handed between the subject and the reader very easily, and these are becoming increasingly popular, particularly among those practitioners who incorporate an element of psychometry into their readings. A crystal ball of approximately five inches in diameter is ideal to enable the reader apparently to lose himself in the crystal while remaining consciously alert throughout. The larger size of crystal ball makes this easier. This process of apparently losing oneself in a completely empty space enables the crystal-gazer to assume a mental and psychic state of being which can bring about a good psychic reading.

AURA READING

If you choose to practise a form of gazing, it is liable to lead to psychic visions. These visions will appear to be seen in the crystal, the water or whatever substance you are gazing at. They are normally preceded by a misty fog which envelops the substance and then, inside that fog, images may appear very clearly. It is even possible in this mist to see discarnate entities, sometimes known as guides. In fact gazing can be a bridge between the reader and one or more guides who may make contact through this medium and give helpful information regarding the reading in question. You can also start to see the aura.

The theosophist C. W. Leadbeater wrote in great detail about the psychic centres, or *chakras*, in his book *The Chakras*,[1] as have many others. Psychic energies enter and leave the aura through the psychic centres as determined by the mental and emotional state of each individual. The physical health of a person can also be seen psychically by assessing the emanations in a person's aura. An aura reader claims to be able to see this psychic body and the different-coloured energies in it, and to analyse the psychic, mental and physical well-being of the subject through this process. This procedure is virtually a focus for the reader's concentration and flow of intuition, and very often it will lead into a divinatory reading about the subject's future.

Most aura readers are not seeing the full aura but are gaining a partial glimpse of it. However, they can still give a very good reading. In some cases they receive intuitive information which manifests to them as certain colours around the subject. Here again there is a link with the practice of psychometry, in that they are tuning in to the aura in order to receive impressions, thoughts and feelings from the subject which can then lead onwards, through using their own intuition, to a glimpse of the person's present and future potential.

It is a strange thing that the more mystical powers you are capable of, sometimes the less you will use them—at least openly. There are many reasons for this, but one is that the more you know, the more you can influence and even control the actions of others. Excessive influence and control over others is harmful to them because it limits their free will to learn from life and gain the experiences for which they were born. The more advanced practitioner knows this and will refrain from doing this.

In a reading of any kind the reader can have a great impact upon a sincere and open-minded subject. The reading will often not only be an indication of the subject's potential and the experiences he or she needs in life, but can also affect and influence the life of the subject. This is one of the reasons why a more advanced practitioner, who is capable, for example, of actually seeing an aura in full, would be very wary of fully using an ability such as this except in most unusual conditions. If the average psychic who uses the method of aura reading was really capable of knowing the aura fully, he would be able to do far more than give a reading for divination purposes. He would know the full and detailed past of the subject which, some people would say, includes their former lifetimes or incarnations.

The old adage 'You don't have to tell all the truth all of the time' is very applicable in this context. Knowledge, after all, is extremely powerful and by giving people information, even about themselves, which they are not really ready to receive, harm can be done rather than good. This often applies to giving supposed details of past lives. In psychic and occult practices, Alexander Pope's famous line 'a little learning is a dangerous thing' is a very valuable yardstick.

OTHER ABSTRACT SYSTEMS

Related to aura reading is the practice of Kirlian photographic readings. Kirlian was a scientist in the Soviet Union who developed a method of photographing the aura. Today this photographic method is used by some people to obtain a photograph of energies around the aura from which a reading can be given. Naturally these photographs do not give a full picture of the aura, although this system has been used to prove that the aura exists. Kirlian photography is certainly worthy of further study and investigation and is a very interesting scientific confirmation of something which has been believed by mystics for many centuries. The effectiveness of readings, though, using this system, depends mainly upon the intuitive ability of the person giving the reading. The Kirlian photographs by themselves would arguably be of limited value without an intuitive reader.

Numerous other systems of divination exist. Some of them are little known outside native communities, but they work very effectively indeed. It is staggering just how many materials can be used to make an analysis of psychic impressions. Sand reading, for example, where a person places the palm of his hand in a bowl of sand and leaves an impression for the reader to analyse, can bring excellent results. Again, this is a rather abstract system, which has little to draw on from a technical point of view, and yet the reader can tap her flow of intuition through practising this method. Another often ridiculed method of divination, tea-leaf reading, can also be exceptionally accurate. I have personally received a tea-leaf reading from a psychic who was able to make some very precise findings through analysing the tea leaves left in my cup after a drink of tea.

It is ultimately the relationship developed by the reader with his or her chosen method that makes the system work. I even know of a person who claims to be able to give readings through noting the number plates on cars as they pass him, when he is walking down the road or sitting in the passenger seat. He has obviously worked out his own code for analysing the numbers and letters on these number plates and has been able to make accurate predictions for people at certain times by observing these number plates while in a psychic state of consciousness. On the surface this seems very eccentric, but really it is no different from any other method used and could be described as a modern version of tea-leaf reading. Naturally, it should not be practised while driving!

PHILOSOPHY BEHIND ABSTRACT METHODS

The philosophy behind crystal-gazing and some of the other methods which are more abstract in concept is, in essence, a very profound one. It is based on what we might call the 'vacuum of life'. This is not in any way related to existentialism, which emerged in the early part of the twentieth century and tended to stress the importance of physical actions because the atheistic existentialists believed there was nothing else real to go by. Although some of the surface characteristics are similar to existentialism, this philosophy of the 'vacuum of life' has its roots in ancient mysticism and has the exact opposite philosophical message to some of the barren materialistic philosophies of the twentieth century.

The philosophy which I have termed the 'vacuum of life' philosophy is based on the principle that nature abhors a vacuum. Indeed, in life there is no such thing as a vacuum. Therefore a vacuum is only theoretically possible. Certainly a vacuum can be created which excludes chemical elements such as oxygen and so forth, but a complete psychic vacuum is a metaphysical impossibility. The mystic therefore concludes that in a theoretical vacuum, which is sometimes referred to as 'nothingness', you would find all things. Nature would abhor this emptiness so much that whatever you demanded would fill the empty space. Some would say that whatever you really needed would then come to you.

This philosophy is very well illustrated in certain Tibetan exercises which are designed to induce meditation. In these practices one is encouraged to negate one's consciousness and suppress the natural flow of thought. Indian yogic writings refer to this flow of thought as 'seeds' and the goal of some Sanskrit writings is to attain the seedless state of consciousness. Here one has to give a very clear health warning. **Without the correct guidance and the correct mental approach, this type of practice can be very dangerous** since it tends to induce a negative mental blankness which might under certain conditions lead to an uncontrolled trance condition. In fact, some people deliberately blank their minds for the very reason that they wish to enter a trance over which they have no control so that they can be taken over by an outside entity or what they believe to be a god, ancestor or benign spirit.

The 'vacuum of life' philosophy does not encourage this at all. One should remain conscious and controlled, while removing all those obstructions to the inner light as it were, which prevent this light from shining in its fullness. This is the goal of certain Taoist practices and is well described by the sage Lao Tzu in the marvellous Chinese text, *Tao Te Ching*.

Systems such as astrology, numerology and the Tarot have specific laws of interpretation which one can draw on without being psychic at all, and this makes them easier to use in the early stages. Many readers use an abstract method in addition to other systems, for example the crystal ball combined with the Tarot. You might start off with a straightforward reading of the Tarot cards based on what you know about them, and then, when psychic impressions start to fill your mind, turn to the crystal ball and use it as a focus to bring these impressions through.

INTUITIVE READINGS

You need to create a conducive atmosphere in which to perform a reading. It is a wonderful thing to have a special room where you can perform readings and indeed any other mystical practices, but this is not always possible. However, you may be able to use a particular corner of a room which will start to gain a certain mystical feeling and power if one uses it purely for these things. This power will in turn help you to perform your mystical practices and readings in that part of the room, because of the atmosphere generated there. The atmosphere can also be enhanced by the use of incense and perfumed oils.

It is very important to obtain the right degree of lighting. There are varying opinions about this. Some advocate near blackness, but I would recommend you to avoid blackness in most mystical exercises, especially in the early stages. In scrying or crystal-gazing the light must be dim in order to try to avoid light reflections in the crystal or other object, and to create an atmosphere in which the crystal itself can virtually take on a psychic light of its own. In any form of psychic gazing you are, by definition, using the eyesight, but you need gradually to make a natural transition from physical viewing to psychic viewing. It is important to eliminate any physical obstructions that stand in the way of that pure space in which psychic expression can take place.

Once the system has been chosen and the atmosphere in the room has been achieved, the reading can commence. Basically there are three presences in the room: the subject, the reader and the system or device which is being used. The subject is active, the reader is receptive and the device is neutral.

The subject may not give you any information verbally— in fact, too much information can interfere with the free flow of your psychic impressions. There is certainly nothing wrong in asking questions of the subject when necessary, but it is best to avoid allowing the subject to give you an extensive amount of information. Incidentally, the information given to a reader by a subject is not always accurate. I am not suggesting that the subject will generally be deliberately dishonest, but quite often his or her memory may be at fault. I remember, for example, a case in which I picked up a psychic impression from a subject about something which had occurred in his early life. The subject completely denied this occurrence. It kept coming back to me and I kept repeating it. It was only after about thirty minutes and my dogged persistence that the subject actually remembered the event in question. This taught me very strongly that one must sometimes listen to one's psychic impressions despite the information one is given by the subject concerned. It would have been tempting in this case just to drop the issue and say it was a wrong impression, but the intuition kept saying otherwise.

When I say that the subject is active I mean that, consciously or unconsciously, he or she is giving information—radiating impressions and vibrations—and the reader who is receptive will receive and analyse these vibrations. You might say that the device or system is completely unnecessary to the whole process and in one sense you would be right, but it acts as a focus. It enables the reader to gain a certain state of consciousness by emptying him- or herself of extraneous conscious thoughts and tapping into a higher aspect of mind—the intuition. It also acts as a symbolic focus for the subject, whether she realises it or not, to emanate the vibrations and impressions which the reader needs to receive.

DEVELOPING INTUITION

No matter how much we talk about different systems, we always come back to the same inherent faculty within us all—intuition. How exactly do we learn to recognise and develop this faculty when using one or more of the systems of divination? The answer is very simple to write, but not always easy to do. Listen whenever your intuition speaks. Do not brush aside impressions received, nor listen to them indiscriminately, but analyse them, note them down and if appropriate discuss them until you reach a point where you start to be able to recognise the difference between a wandering thought and a definite intuitive prompting.

It is a strange human quirk that many people expect their psychic faculty to be something that requires no work or effort. You either have it or you don't—if you do, you were born with it, if you don't then you will never get it. This kind of reasoning prevents the active development of our intuitive faculty which can only be cultivated through diligent and careful open-minded practice, with patience.

I have found, both with myself and others who are developing their psychic powers, that it is necessary to have a degree of humility in all you do. This prevents a fanatical self-righteousness which can easily lead to mistakes being made in one's interpretation. Another great quality to maintain when developing psychically, strange as it may sound, is a sense of humour. There is nothing worse than developing psychics who take themselves too seriously. In the early stages you are going to make mistakes, so it is necessary to be as undogmatic as possible and retain the ability to take these mistakes in your stride. A sense of humour greatly helps with this and avoids you going to the other extreme of giving up the whole thing completely just because you have got something wrong. It is essential to be able to admit when you are wrong but never give up.

Another very useful tip to remember is the importance of doing these practices in a friendly atmosphere, especially when you are starting out. This may sound rather obvious but it is more important than it may seem. In an unfriendly, tense atmosphere it is difficult to relax mentally and therefore to allow the free flow of intuitive thought. It is ideal to practise this with others who are also trying to develop their psychic abilities and therefore have an understanding and empathy for your situation. When you start to receive psychic impressions, which can often come in mental bursts at considerable speed, you will gradually start to assimilate what you are receiving. A blank spell when really nothing seems to come at all may be followed by a rush of impressions and information, and one often has to discuss these to interpret them. In the right atmosphere others can help you to do this.

The importance of interpretation cannot be stressed too much. An exact psychic impression misinterpreted is at best useless, at worse misleading. By adopting a friendly, humble and yet determined approach, you gradually learn to discriminate between your faculty of intuition and those imaginative wanderings and subconscious impressions which also go on within us.

5
The Inner Eye

*

One of the keys to developing psychic ability is the control and use of the imagination. The sceptic may say that all psychic ability is a result of imagination. His assumption will be that imagination is something contrary to the truth and that reason is something synonymous with the truth, but this is not always so.

Uncontrolled imagination can be dangerous. But it is only through the controlled use of our imagination that we glimpse what is possible to us and to others. It is this glimpse of what is possible that gives us the opportunity to attain it. If a person never imagined he could be a writer, he would never write; if a person never imagined she could cook a good meal, she would never be a good cook, and so on and so on. The same is definitely true of using imagination in our psychic development, providing always that we use it in a controlled manner.

IMAGINATION

Reason alone, without the imaginative flair that characterises great thinking, is bland and not necessarily accurate. The writings of the ancient Greek philosophers, for example, while being a brilliant demonstration of the inherent rational

THE INNER EYE 73

capacity of the human mind, also contain many factual errors and inaccurate theories. Of course they were teaching against the background of an ancient religion which had degenerated into fear, superstition and man-made concepts of how the gods behave. The logical prowess of Socrates, Plato, Aristotle and others was not only a breath of fresh air at the time but became one of the intellectual bases for the western world. More than this, it was a demonstration of the potential mental attributes of man, as distinct from the unpredictable 'gods' who by that time had been debased with some of the more unattractive human qualities such as jealousy, possessiveness, anger and revenge.

However, in the view of many people, civilisation has been too heavily influenced by this rational outpouring from the minds of the great ancient Greek thinkers. It is interesting to note that the father of much of Greek philosophy is believed to have been Pythagoras, a very underestimated mystic with a deep interest in the psychic sciences. His name literally means 'the voice of Apollo', which some have interpreted as 'medium for Apollo'. He is reputed to have led a mystical school which was considered far more important than the geometrical theorem for which he is now famous in modern mathematics. His disciple, Socrates, taught Plato who, in turn, taught Aristotle who was, in turn, the tutor of Alexander the Great. Note how each successive generation moved farther away from the mystical roots of Pythagoras' original teaching. Some metaphysical thinkers believe that Pythagoras himself was a Master connected with hidden spiritual retreats around the earth, where other Masters dwell and work in secret. Those Masters are normally referred to as the Spiritual Hierarchy of Earth or, more colloquially, the Great White Brotherhood.

There is certainly a move now away from the purely rational and deductive, back to some of the more mystical qualities which Pythagoras first taught, before his more famous successor philosophers became known. As Greek philosophy moved farther away from mysticism and more towards pure reason, so the philosophy became arguably less and less spiritual. Indeed it culminated in Alexander's imperialistic campaigns to instil Greek culture in as many people as possible by invading and suppressing them. This action in itself would have been in direct opposition to the teaching of Pythagoras. Perhaps this illustrates the danger of straying too far from the safe harbour of mystical principles and into the precarious waters of unfettered rational deduction.

A more complete approach to philosophy might have maintained the rigours of logical discipline, but also allowed the mind to embrace higher aspects which themselves can produce a deeper spiritual realisation. Since our modern educational system is largely derived from classical principles which originated in ancient Greece, this is very relevant today. Reason is essential to all forms of learning, but on its own it is limited. Imagination is a quality which, if developed, can open up vast new horizons of realisation and attainment, but it needs reason to control it. It is not just a mental attribute which invents unreal thoughts and pictures. It is a faculty which, if controlled, can bring a greatly enhanced awareness of many aspects of life. It can lead us towards a deep understanding of things which hitherto were concealed from us, because it will furnish our logic with the thoughts, ideas and information it needs to understand life more fully.

VISUALISATION EXERCISES

Carefully balanced visualisation exercises are an excellent example of controlled imagination and can be extremely valuable to the psychic practitioner. There are two definite guidelines which I would recommend before practising any visualisation. The first is that **the visualisation should be as positive as possible in all ways**. This may sound obvious, but if you are not careful you can allow negativity to creep into a visualisation almost without realising it. For example, if you are visualising a very pleasant country scene with undulating hills, blue skies, a gentle breeze and the pleasant aroma of flowers, you may find that a black cloud suddenly comes across the skies. There may even be a thunderclap, lightning and winds marring the beauty of this picturesque visualisation. This in itself may signify psychically some event which is due to arise or some feelings within the individual performing the visualisation. Alternatively, it may just be a result of uncontrolled imagination. Even if this change of scene from a beautiful day to a miserable one is informative to you, it is still important mentally to turn the visualisation back into the positive, picturesque scene you first visualised. By doing so you will be gaining control over your imaginative faculty.

If your visualisation includes water, such as a river, a lake or the sea, and the water becomes very rough, again this may well signify an occurrence due to take place in your life or in the life of the person or subject that is on your mind at the time. This can be the beginnings of your reception of psychic information, and can lead into far more specific and revealing information as you progress with your visualisation practices. However, no matter where these visualisations lead you, it is always important to end them in a positive way. Bring the sea, the lake or the ocean back to a calm state again before concluding the visualisation practice. In this way you will start to gain control over the visualisation rather than allowing it to control you.

The second guideline to be aware of before practising visualisations is that **they should never be used to interfere with other people's free will**. In fact it is safest not to include other people in your visualisations at all, especially in the early stages. Of course, healing can be sent to other people, but even then I would advise you not to visualise them with their sickness, because you are then only mentally affirming this illness through visualisation, even though your motive is to send healing. There are specific practices which involve the visualisation of advanced people, such as Saints and Masters, but these should only be practised after receiving guidance from an expert in the metaphysical sciences.

One of the simplest and most effective visualisations is often taught in slightly differing versions in yoga and other development workshops and classes. It is known simply as 'filling the aura'. You should visualise the aura as an ovoid or egg-shaped body several inches away from the physical body each side all around you. For the purpose of this visualisation practice you should imagine this egg-shaped aura initially as transparent and not conditioned with any particular colour. The reason for this is that there are many colours intermingling in the aura, which are the energies coursing through the psychic centres and psychic channels both from within you and from without you, and you cannot possibly know the exact colour formation in your aura. Therefore if you see, virtually, a transparent aura you are not introducing any particular colour or colours which might, in fact, be erroneous.

Having visualised the aura around you, you gradually start to visualise or imagine this blank, transparent egg-shaped form being illuminated, as though a light has been turned on within you. The aura virtually starts to shine from within. This takes place not only on the outside of your physical body but right the way through your physical body as well. The whole of your being, including both your body and this psychic shell around the body, is shining with a vibrant white illumination. You virtually become an egg-shaped light bulb. You imagine this so strongly that if anyone were to walk into the room where you are sitting you feel that they would immediately see this tremendous illumination around you.

This practice is both safe and beneficial. It indicates that the higher part of your nature, which some would call the soul, is illuminating your mental, physical and psychic being. In the process you are mentally and emotionally lifted upwards. The effect of this should be to enhance your mental inspiration and bring about a more positive approach to life. If done regularly it should make you a more dynamic and magnetic person. It will also tend to make you more aware of your aura, so that you will gradually start to feel it around you and the energies passing through it.

In order to perform this or any other visualisation correctly, you should make sure that you are in a room alone or in a country location where you will not be disturbed and can therefore perform the entire practice without interruption. Although it is extremely simple, this practice does require considerable concentration to perform it correctly and to ensure that the whole of your being is illuminated. You may experience a certain psychological resistance to this illumination taking place. This resistance might come from a more negative part of your nature either arguing against you doing the practice or emotionally trying to prevent you from doing it. If this should happen, follow the yogic dictum that the best time to do a spiritual or psychic practice is when you least want to, as that is when it sometimes works most effectively for you.

This is a typical example of a practice in which you are using your imagination not to invent something false, but to make you more aware of something true. The aura really does exist, and through the power of imagination you can start to make some contact with it. In fact, imagination can take you closer to reality than reason in certain respects.

Gradually, by performing a practice like this one, and any other good visualisation exercises, you will start to enhance your psychic vision. You will start to open your 'mind's eye' and move your visualisation beyond the purely physical. There will come a state when you no longer need to use your imagination because by then you will have bridged the gap between theory and fact. By using your imagination initially, you can start to discover the reality of your psychic nature.

When you first do this practice it will be a purely mental exercise. But gradually you should start to feel and even psychically see part or all of the aura around you. You should not allow your visualisation to wander away from the initial goal of illuminating your aura. Ideally you should make sure you do not finish this practice without having filled the entire aura around you. Incidentally, some people find it helpful to keep a diary or a record of their visualisation exercises and thereby chart their progress. Sometimes these practices can be extremely uplifting, and sometimes not—sometimes they can even be disturbing. Whatever reaction you get, you should take it in a balanced and unemotional way. By keeping a diary, you will start to see and note your development as it takes place.

When you start to practise these things you will learn about your own capacity to visualise. One could talk about riding a bike for several weeks, describing the motion of the wheels, exactly how to sit on the seat and the different nervous sensations which go on within the physical body as you ride. It would be a highly complex study in advanced biology to describe this fully. But it would only take a matter of hours for most people to learn how to ride a bike and to start to do it. It is only then that you really understand how to get from point A to point B on a bicycle. Visualisation is very similar to this. When you start to do it you realise many things about yourself and your own capacity, which will teach you more than reading a dozen books on the subject.

You will probably find, at times, that your mind wanders from the original point of the visualisation. You might even, on occasions, get lost in a visualisation and sidetracked from your original purpose. It is then that you need to use your concentration to bring you back to the main task at hand, without forcing yourself unduly, but nevertheless applying a certain mental discipline. Practice always makes perfect in this respect, and some discipline is essential to all forms of personal development.

Prior to performing your chosen visualisation, it would be a good thing to practise the watchfulness I described in the first chapter. When, through this watchfulness, you have induced a physically relaxed but mentally alert condition and are becoming more aware of yourself and your thoughts, you can then start your visualisation. You will gradually find that you have the ability to place a virtual mental demand on what it is you are trying to bring about. In the visualisation of your aura, it will be as though you were turning on a dimmer light on a lighting console, which gradually illuminates and fills the whole of your aura with light. This practice, if done regularly, will gradually start to awaken your capacity for psychic vision or clairvoyance through the power of controlled imagination.

It is a strange fact that, in the context of psychic development, some people feel that imagination is unhealthy and only leads to a fantasy state. And yet in all branches of the arts they fully accept it as being absolutely essential. It is also used in the commercial world. What are the advertising teams doing if not using their imagination to try and sell their products? What are designers doing if not using their imagination to come up with something that will actually be appealing to people? In visualisations, providing they are balanced, positive and controlled, you are using imagination to bridge a gap between yourself and a metaphysical reality. You will reach a stage where you will not require imagination to see clairvoyantly or receive psychic impressions.

You may find that you have certain experiences and are unsure whether they are imagination or psychic happenings. In a case like this I would advise you to keep your feet very firmly on the ground and not jump to any conclusions until you really know for sure what you are dealing with. Again, there is no harm in keeping an open mind about things like this, but I would certainly advise you not to make outlandish claims, as unfortunately some tend to do. Later on, if you persist with these practices, you will start to go beyond any grey areas of doubt about your psychic experiences into tangible and provable events which will be confirmed in a very precise way.

There is a host of visualisation practices available in books and tapes. Some of these do not attempt to visualise something which really exists, such as the aura, but rather to create an imaginary scene that will benefit your mind and your body. Remarkable demonstrations have been made, for example, by individuals sitting indoors with curtains drawn, who by visualising sunlight have actually gained a physical sun tan. Others have improved their health by visualising a rejuvenating, healthy outdoor environment. Usually the results will be less spectacular than this, but a visualisation of your favourite country location can bring you a wonderful feeling of well-being. By visualising a country scene which is conducive to your emotional and physical desire for peace, relaxation, tranquillity or just a natural uplift, you can improve your state of being.

I am not advocating here a form of escapism from reality or any attempt to believe that you are physically in this country location. You will know full well all the time that you are only performing a visualisation practice, but what you are really doing is introducing into your psychic and mental environment certain energies that are invoked by the visualisation you are performing and which are beneficial to you.

It is vital when performing such a practice that you decide what you are going to include in your visualisation and do not allow your imagination or your subconscious mind to dictate to you what will appear. There is a tremendous difference between performing a visualisation practice and daydreaming. Daydreaming is a vague, haphazard thing that takes you over, virtually, almost uninvited. You can allow yourself to slip into a daydream without determining its outcome. A visualisation, on the other hand, is predetermined, and is usually based on a tried and tested method taught by a qualified teacher who fully understands his subject. You decide to do it in the conditions that you choose, for the length of time that you determine. The main purpose behind this whole procedure is to start to gain control over your imagination and use it in the way that you choose to do.

As with divination, the key to finding a suitable set of visualisations and techniques for personal development is to follow a system that is attractive and helpful to you. If you follow one of the systems taught by one of the teachers of yoga referred to in the first chapter, you will not be misled. There are also several modern meditations, contemplations and visualisations available from New Age groups, some of which are most effective. Here you need to apply discrimination, above all avoiding anything that is not fundamentally positive in nature.

It is an error to assume that because a practice is old it is therefore good. You can pick up a number of books purporting to be of Tibetan, Egyptian or some other origin which are in fact most undesirable. You can also be subtly invited to participate in a white magical ritual which, on closer investigation, turns out to be nothing of the sort. Common sense is the best guide in all these things. Providing the practice is not harmful to you or to anyone else, is entirely positive and does not attempt to interfere with anyone else's free will, you will safely discover by practising it whether or not it is helpful to you in your psychic development and in your life in general.

CLAIRVOYANCE

Regular practice of a balanced set of visualisations will bring you many benefits, but the main one is the gradual awakening of the inner eye, which is a term used to denote the 'third eye' or Christ centre. This centre is situated in the aura, just above the bridge of the nose and between the eyebrows. When you are practising clairvoyance you should not assume that you have opened this psychic centre in its entirety, as some books would suggest. You may be seeing a reflection of this inner eye, but in fact are activating lower psychic centres than that.

In deciding which psychic sense to concentrate on, whether it be psychic seeing, psychic hearing or another psychic sense, the choice is a very personal one. In some ways it is similar to the arts: some are more attracted to visual representation through paintings, sculpture and so forth, others to the aural sense through music. People are generally attracted to both in different degrees, and it is good to include both these main senses of psychic seeing and psychic hearing to a greater or lesser extent. But usually an individual will have a particular flair in one direction or another. In fact, the old wives' tale about having a 'sixth sense' is not a correct definition of psychic ability. It would be more correct to say that we have five psychic senses complementing the five basic physical senses.

Clairvoyance has two separate meanings, both of which are associated with vision. The first is divination and the second is the ability to have psychic vision through seeing objects and occurrences on a different psychic level of existence. At its height the 'third eye' is capable of something far greater than clairvoyance—a deep knowledge and wisdom about whatever you choose to meditate upon—but that is at an advanced stage of development, which only a few attempt to manifest.

Clairvoyance will give us a much much fuller appreciation of life as a whole, but it is only a step along the journey, not the final destination. Seeing the aura, the energies of life or *pranas*, and intelligences who are not incarnate in physical bodies because they have passed through death, will give the clairvoyant a much broader vision of the totality of all things, but not give the ultimate knowledge of life's purpose. In my opinion some clairvoyants have got stuck at this level instead of learning and moving onwards. This is a danger we need to watch out for very carefully. We should never be fully satisfied with the stage of progress we have reached.

It is interesting to note that in some Mystery Schools the students were actually taught to reject psychic development entirely. If psychic visions occurred they were told to detach from them mentally and concentrate purely on the programme of meditations and austerities that they were undergoing. There was some sense in this in that the ultimate goal of these students was not so much clairvoyance as to gain a deep knowledge about the purpose of life itself. However, in my view, it is an unfortunate teaching to propound nowadays, because we can learn very much along the way by developing our clairvoyance, even though at some later stage we shall have to move on from this if we wish to attain full enlightenment. The experience of clairvoyance can be an essential stepping-stone and, more importantly, can be used to help others.

MEDIUMS

There is a complete rejection of clairvoyance by some orthodox religious establishments which have a fear of psychic awareness in general, unless it comes through the official channels of the establishment in question and is interpreted in an orthodox way. Seers and prophets, not to mention healers and mediums, are generally regarded with suspicion by the orthodox thinker, sometimes until centuries after their death when they are belatedly recognised as great religious figures and, in certain cases, are even canonised!

There are mediums who make contact with fairly ordinary guides (people who have physically passed on) and make the dangerous mistake of overestimating the wisdom and spiritual stature of these guides. This, too, can lead to errors and limit the development of these mediums. The guides may be good people, possibly relatives or other people compatible with them, who are able to overshadow them and pass on information psychically. Sometimes this can be helpful and sometimes not. There is no reason to believe that just because you are in touch with guides, they know all there is to know about life. In certain respects they may know less than you, in others they may know considerably more. But they are unlikely, in most cases, to be exceptionally advanced people and it would be a misjudgement to take all their words as fact, as some mediums sadly do, just because they come from higher realms of existence.

I have personally come across a number of psychics and mediums who have done just this. They listen indiscriminately to what they are told by their guides and pass it on as dogmatic fact. If they do this, they are just as flawed as any establishment or organisation which passes on unquestioned dogma. Furthermore, it is possible that the medium has made a mistake in his or her reception of some of the information from these guides; that, too, is not often questioned by mediums or many of the people who listen to them. The end result of this can be misguidance instead of guidance.

There are cases in which mediums bring through guidance which is accurate but, to be frank, paltry in significance. It might be a genuine demonstration of psychic reception, but it is not valuable material. Somehow intelligent discrimination seems to go out of the window with some people when they are on the receiving end of psychic material. When we develop, we have to guard against the ego creeping in and tempting us to believe that whatever comes through us is highly elevated. It may be good information, but it is not infallibly correct unless we ourselves are Masters in the mystic sciences and our guides are also Masters, a situation which is extremely rare.

These warnings aside, clairvoyance is an educational and exciting adventure which is well worth pursuing. It opens up literally new vistas of experience which, with the help of careful discrimination, can be highly revealing. Some of those who profess their opposition to occultism, divination and psychic development often describe with great enthusiasm what are tantamount to psychic experiences of their own. They do not refer to them as such, but that is indeed what they are. If, for example, a person claims to have seen Jesus at her right hand, or to be able to 'speak in tongues', which as far as she is concerned is the Spirit speaking through her, these are psychic experiences. In effect there is very little difference between this type of claim and the claims that psychics make, except that the psychic does not normally attribute her source to Jesus or the Spirit, and usually this is far more sensible than the rather extreme claims that some people make.

VISIONS

Visions are extremely interesting phenomena which can be highly uplifting or, in certain cases, disturbing. It is possible to have a wonderful vision of Jesus Christ, Saint Peter, the Lord Buddha, Sri Krishna or another elevated Being. It is also possible to have a demonic type of vision on which it would not be advisable to concentrate. However, from an analytical point of view these visions, whether of the uplifting, spiritual kind or the opposite, do not necessarily denote an encounter with the entity you believe you have seen. You may not actually have come into contact with the person or Being about whom you have had the vision. Either might be a product of your own inner thoughts and feelings personified by a particular Being and all that that Being means to you. This would then be a product of your higher imagination, manifesting itself as a vision. Of course, I am not ruling out the possibility that a great Being has come into your presence, which has happened at certain times throughout history, but even if this is not the case, please do not think that the vision was a delusion or an unimportant experience. It may have been virtually a way for your higher nature to speak to you through this vision. It is in effect your link with a higher aspect of your mind.

Visions can be associated with a particular metaphysical path or school of learning that you may be pursuing. For example, there are certain schools of yoga that give particular advice regarding visions of symbolic entities which represent certain forces, energies or even philosophical concepts. These forces, energies or concepts are being manifested in visionary form. In Kaballistic magic the manifestation of certain entities or archangels can take place when they are invoked by the practitioner using certain rituals, and they may then be seen in the person's mind's eye or imagination. These represent certain forces or energies which will help that person or any others he is helping through the ritual, provided they are used correctly.

Some visions may be purely symbolic, and certain people have a much greater tendency to see symbols than others. These may be famous symbols with which we are all familiar, or they may be symbols that you have never encountered before. I met someone who had frequent symbolic visions and was staggered to find, when looking them up in an encyclopaedia of symbology, that he was seeing symbols which had a precise meaning, although he had never consciously come across them in his life before. This type of vision can be most intriguing and revealing. The reason why a vision comes to a person in symbolic form might be because it requires deeper thought and interpretation by the individual. It virtually forces that individual to think more deeply about it. The meanings are obviously complex and profound and very often require deeper meditation or contemplation to understand them fully.

Sometimes one can tune in psychically to a virtual fund of psychic material which is associated with a particular metaphysical or mystical system. This may appear to you in visionary form, even before you have consciously come across it. You are tuning in to a whole source of material which you are then drawing upon and acquainting yourself with at a visionary level. This happened to me when I started to practise the Tarot. I had the most extraordinary series of visions. On one occasion I saw in my room psychically a bandaged figure who was completely still and yet was a somewhat eerie sight. He was most unpleasant and rather chilling and yet although there was an eerieness about him, no vibration seemed to be emanated by or through him. On studying a catalogue of Tarot packs some days later (at that time I was looking into dozens of alternative packs to find a suitable one to use), I saw in one of them this exact figure printed on a card—in a pack I did not choose to purchase, incidentally. I had never seen this pack before, and yet this figure had appeared to me in visionary form a few days earlier.

I realise now that I was so immersed at that time in the mind emanations of the Tarot in general that I was starting to tune in to those ancient energies associated with Tarot. I was actually receiving impressions in visionary form from that fund of metaphysical knowledge we might call the Tarot thought-form. When one performs a Tarot reading, as well as divining one is invoking indirectly certain energies associated with this Tarot thought-form, which has evolved through the centuries, enhanced for better or worse by all those who have applied their thoughts and energies and visualisations to it.

INHABITANTS OF OTHER REALMS

As well as the visions I have described here, there are examples of clairvoyance where one sees people who are psychically present. They are not alive in physical bodies but have passed on to other realms and can return to visit under certain conditions in astral form. The first time I experienced such a vision I thought I was imagining it, and in a sense I was, but I realised later that I had been using the faculty of imagination to see something real, instead of something unreal.

A very famous psychic told me that she started out as the assistant of another medium who used to give public demonstrations. One day the medium was taken ill and she, as his assistant, was asked to fill the gap. She did not regard herself as a developed psychic so in desperation she just started to use her imagination, virtually to invent things and see what happened. Some would say this was fraudulent, and on the face of it it was. But to her amazement she found that her imagination, far from inventing things, was psychically tuning in to real facts about members of the audience, who were shaken to discover her extremely accurate insight into their lives. She was capable of psychically picking up things about people, their relatives, their problems, their health and so forth. This illustrates the fact that we have to use our imagination to bring forth our own latent psychic abilities.

This is of course a very rare case and I would not advocate that you attempt to do this. Undoubtedly she had unknowingly developed her psychic abilities while working as the medium's assistant. But it does illustrate the connection between our faculty of imagination and our innate psychic ability which can be awakened by a controlled and discriminating use of the imagination. In psychic development we need to move through imagination into real ESP.

My first definite experience of clairvoyantly seeing a person of the other realms happened when I was staying in the house of a woman in Australia. One day, as I sat in her lounge, I saw in my mind's eye a young lady dressed in the clothes of the 1940s. When I started to describe what I was psychically seeing to my hostess, she registered great surprise. The psychic vision I was having was accompanied by a word which I also passed on to my hostess. This turned out to be the nickname of a close friend of hers who had died during the Second World War. The description was too perfect to ignore and the nickname was one I had never heard before. It was so unusual it could not have been a coincidental guess. As often happens with such experiences, it was only afterwards that the whole event seemed strange. I virtually had to pinch myself to see whether it had actually happened. But at the time it seemed completely natural and quite a normal occurrence.

In this adventure of psychic unfoldment one is constantly learning to discriminate in order to identify between a controlled psychic vision which is grounded in truth, and a vague, imaginative wandering which at its worst can be a dangerous delusion. Here let me stress again that **anyone who is prone to mental illness would not be advised to attempt to practise psychic development until he or she has stabilised the condition under the correct medical supervision**.

When starting to develop clairvoyance, you should resist the temptation to make dogmatic claims. Keep an open mind, just as you request others to do, until you have developed far enough to be able to analyse exactly what has transpired. All these experiences are only feelings. They can be extremely valuable and informative, in some cases more valuable and informative than mere rational deduction, but they are not absolute knowledge.

Psychic vision will also lead to a far greater appreciation of the colour which permeates all life. This is not the place to go into the subject of Colour Healing, about which many books have been written, save to say that it really does work. Psychic colours play a major part in bringing about any form of healing because the aura, as mentioned earlier, is composed of different colours and needs those colours in balance in order to be healthy, which then reflects on the mind and body. This does not only apply to Colour Healing, but also to what you wear, how you decorate your house or office and even the colour of the food you eat. If you start to develop clairvoyance, I would strongly recommend you to study the whole subject of colour and what effect these colours have on us all.

The inner eye, when fully developed, can see at least as clearly as the physical eyes. The visions can be as definite as anything physical. It is always necessary to turn back to the faculty of intuition to interpret your visions. Sometimes it can take years before you really understand the true meaning of a particular psychic experience. No matter how clairvoyant you become, no matter how clairaudient or what mediumistic abilities you may develop, there is no more valuable psychic attribute to any of us than our intuition which, if we have the courage and faith to follow it, will never lead us astray. The intuition will virtually act as a guiding light to help us use our psychic abilities correctly.

6

The Inner Ear

*

When you actually start to receive information from those who have passed on, and this information is substantiated in one way or another, any doubts you may have about life after death will quickly disappear. Mediumship is not as safe a method as clairaudience because mediumship involves some form of trance. Unless you are adept in the practice of yoga or another branch of metaphysics, an element of risk is introduced, since you will not be in full control of the trance condition you are using. In the practice of clairaudience, on the other hand, you can maintain full control and be conscious of what is going on around you while, at the same time, tuning in to your psychic sense of hearing.

TRANCE MEDIUMSHIP

Mediumship in one form or another has been practised in most cultures and civilisations throughout history, and still is today. It is the method through which people on other planes communicate directly with people on the physical plane of existence. Briefly, there is more than one vibrational plane of existence upon earth. You and I are inhabiting the physical plane at the present time. When our physical body dies, the aura, the astral body, the mind and the soul all continue on another plane of existence. To link up these different planes, a system of trance mediumship can be used. This brief analysis would be generally accepted by a whole variety of metaphysical groups around the world.

If you were an adept in the mystic sciences, you would be able to gain a full control over whatever mediumistic trance condition you decided to use. Since most of us are not adepts, we cannot gain this full and complete control over the mediumistic state. No doubt some mediums would strongly disagree with me, but I would say that at best the average medium has only a partial control over the mediumistic trance state. They might have a considerable ability in mediumship, and they may well bring very accurate and helpful results to many people, but there is still an element of negation (as opposed to control) of a certain part of the conscious mind in order to enter the mediumistic trance state.

Adepts would be able to raise their consciousness to such a high level that they would virtually enter a superconscious state without deliberately negating the conscious mind *per se*. They would have transcended normal consciousness as opposed to blanking it out. But a lesser practitioner would not be able to do this without a blanking out process. To the degree that a negation of the conscious faculty takes place, so the element of control over the trance state is reduced.

This can be clearly seen in a whole range of people from different cultures who enter these trances in order to act as mediums for guides, entities or what they might even refer to as gods. The Tibetans, for example, to this very day often use mediums in order to identify the location of a reincarnated soul whom they consider to be important or advanced, such as the abbot of a monastery or the leader of a particular sect of Buddhism. These mediums, who very often are not Buddhist monks themselves, are approached by monks in order to identify where exactly the reincarnated soul is now dwelling, who his parents are and so forth. The medium then enters a trance condition over which he might have very little control, and probably no memory afterwards of what was said while he was in trance. In this trance state questions are asked of the communicating entity and sometimes detailed descriptions of young children in distant parts of Tibet, who, it is claimed, are specific reincarnated abbots or lamas, will be located. It is uncanny how accurately the entities communicating through these mediums are able to pinpoint, in exact locations in remote areas, children whom the medium could not possibly have known anything about.

The native American indians also used, and probably still do, trance conditions to gain a mediumistic rapport with dis-carnate guides. It appears from spiritualistic findings that American indian guides are among the most common guides who are willing to help assist those living on the physical plane of existence. This may well be because of their long-standing traditions of maintaining a close rapport between those who are living on this physical earth and those who are on a higher realm around the earth. In some of the tribes of Northern America this interchange of information between the planes goes back through many generations.

Other native tribes, from Africa to Asia to South America to the Pacific Islands, have used some form of mediumship. I do not wish to detract from the accuracy of these mediums when I say that there is an element of negation of the conscious mind taking place in their trance conditions. This negation automatically blanks out some of the control that they have over the state, and often means that the mediums do not know what is going on while they are in trance, and often cannot recall what was said afterwards.

I know of cases where people have successfully practised mediumship using a semiconscious trance condition. They have found that although the results of the mediumship were very good and helpful in every way, this practice, over a period of time, started to undermine their own willpower. By constantly allowing others to take them over, even partially, and hence giving up some of their sense of will and control over their consciousness to guides on a frequent basis, a certain undermining was taking place of their mental capacity and they became mentally weaker as a result.

I have many friends who are involved in various forms of psychic practice. I well remember one very good lady who performed excellent healing while in a mediumistic state and indeed, while being overshadowed by guides, was able to play the piano in a way she could not normally play it. However, she was not balanced in her approach to mediumship, and as she grew older started to enter this trance state more and more frequently, sometimes almost haphazardly, until she became very impractical about her daily living habits. She reached the point where she was not sufficiently motivated to have a hole in the roof of her house repaired until asked to do so by a guide! This is the type of imbalance which uncontrolled mediumship can lead to unless you keep your feet very firmly on the physical and conscious ground beneath you.

We do not need to look beyond the shores of the British Isles for great demonstrations of spiritualistic mediumship, which has flourished here for well over a century. The spiritualist movement took off in the late nineteenth century and was supported by well-known figures in literary and scientific circles, including the author Sir Arthur Conan Doyle, the scientist Sir Oliver Lodge, and many others. For those who doubt spiritualism and the proof it provides about life after death, I would strongly recommend a visit to the British Library, which comes under the British Museum. In this library you can study literally hundreds of past spiritualistic journals, such as *The Two Worlds*, and find case after case of substantiated evidence of contact with the deceased. I did this myself, not so much for the purpose of proof, but just out of pure interest.

The question of whether spiritualism is a good thing is an entirely different one. Certainly it has helped many people who were suffering from the sad loss of relatives recently passed on. I myself have been able to bring comfort and encouragement to several in this situation, without mediumistic trance, by clairaudiently making contact with their deceased family. Apart from giving emotional relief regarding their specific loss, it does comfort people to know generally that there is no such thing as death of the soul and mind of the person, and that their close ones still exist in another sphere. However, when it becomes a habit to maintain a relationship with a departed friend or relative through a medium for weeks, months or even years, not for the purpose of comprehending the journey of life from one realm to another but purely for emotional reasons, then in my opinion it is highly questionable. Quite apart from the dangers of entering the trance state necessary to bring through a discarnate entity mediumistically, I have other misgivings about such a practice.

At worst, when the conscious mind is being completely blanked out, the trance state can lead to such things as possession or even mental infirmity. But the process of mediumship has other inherent dangers attached to it. Death is understood in different ways by people of different persuasions, but whatever your views about it are, it is obviously intended, if you believe in any form of destiny, for the person who has passed on to actually move on. If regular contact is maintained with such a person by living relatives through a medium, that process of moving on is held back.

To the relatives or friends here on earth, regular contact with the deceased can become something akin to an emotional addiction, which does not help them adjust to a life without the deceased person. While it may help them just after a passing to come to terms with their grief and understand that there is no such thing as finite death, it is not something which should be maintained over a lengthy period of time. It should not be regarded, for instance, as like making a telephone call to someone who lives in a distant country.

There are cases where a mediumistic contact can be very illuminating and helpful, not so much for emotional reasons, but more for intellectual or spiritual ones. The way to assess the value of a particular demonstration of mediumship is simply to analyse the content of the information received. Such information should be valuable, whether or not it was supplied by a person on the other realms. If a medium or psychic is receiving from somebody who has passed on information which is in itself worthy of study and is thoroughly helpful, then that is very different from mediumship for the purposes of maintaining an emotional relationship. The help given will not be of a selfish or purely personal nature, but will be general and applicable to many situations.

I would recommend clairaudience as a much safer method for gaining contact with people on higher spheres, who wish to give helpful and useful guidance. With clairaudience you have full and complete control over the practice you are undertaking. In a sense a medium is subordinating his or her will to that of the communicator, and even though the communication in some cases is very good and in every way friendly and helpful, a loss of mental drive and purpose may be felt later by the medium who uses this method.

I am not referring in any of this to the advanced yogic state of mediumship, know in the East as *Samadhi*, which can only be successfully attained by a Master in this practice. A great exponent of this state is His Eminence Dr George King, who has lectured extensively on trance and life after death. Some of these lectures are available in tape-recorded form and I thoroughly recommend them for study.[1] He has achieved full control over the state of *Samadhi* on hundreds of occasions.

Lesser states than this, however, require anything from a partial to a complete negation of conscious mental control in order to be taken over by the communicating entity. The reason for this is that the operation of the conscious mind is an obstacle to the psychic entity who wishes to overshadow your consciousness, and unless you are able to tap the full powers of your superconsciousness, as for example in the Samadhic trance referred to, then a partial mental vacuum is left by you for an outside entity to occupy. Once this mental vacuum has been created, an overshadowing entity can use it exactly as it chooses. In extreme cases, such as certain tribal rites where alcohol, sex and even animal sacrifices are used to encourage the medium, native doctor or priest of the tribe to enter the trance state, the condition used may be extremely dangerous. Almost an entire mental vacuum is created within the person. He or she can then be 'taken over' by whatever entity so chooses, and judging by some of the rituals performed in these tribes, the entity is not a very pleasant or positive one. It is foolish to dismiss such rites and ceremonies as meaningless nonsense—in certain cases powerful magic is performed on these occasions. But they are certainly dangerous, and can attract malicious and evil entities to overshadow the blanked-out mind of the medium, or even cause the medium to become mentally deranged.

I have met victims of negative trance, who have attempted to commune with the deceased or even perform other practices which involved blanking out the mind and with it part of the will. Some of these have become fully or partially possessed. There is sometimes a narrow dividing line between mental illness and psychic delusion. It is rare to find a psychologist who really understands psychic events, or indeed a psychic practitioner who is willing to acknowledge the value of psychological balance and discipline. But in reality the two should cooperate together, for many psychological illnesses are related to both psychological disturbance and psychic interference.

Incidentally, the mental vacuum I referred to in relation to blanking out the mind is a very different thing from the 'vacuum of life' philosophy I described in chapter 4, in relation to psychic gazing. In fact in many ways it is the opposite. In gazing, you should not enter any trance condition but remain alert and focused upon an apparent vacuum which is then filled by the psychic and intuitive information you need to give the reading.

CLAIRAUDIENCE

As with all forms of psychic ability, clairaudience is the result of attunement. It is the ability to attune your hearing to that which is beyond the physical, just as with clairvoyance where you are attuning your vision or inner eye to that which is beyond the purely physical. If you practise one of the sciences of divination already described, such as astrology, numerology and so on, these will form the basic structure from which you can allow your interpretive and intuitive abilities to flow. Gradually there will come a stage when, in addition to the deductive procedures involved in analysing a particular subject, along the set guidelines you have learned, impressions will also start to flow to you. One of the ways these impressions can come to you is through psychic hearing.

When you start to awaken the inner ear you will actually start to hear, in your 'mind's ear' as it were, thoughts expressed. Through clairaudience, a communicating entity can enter your consciousness and speak to you. In the early stages this can be a difficult thing to practise, but it is a practice built on very firm foundations because you are conscious throughout the procedure, and therefore in control of the whole thing with full memory recall afterwards. It can lead to an accurate and informative rapport with a guide or other communicator from a higher realm.

A good example of this happened to me several years ago. I was overheard in a restaurant by a woman at another table while I was discussing life after death with a friend. She approached me after the meal and told me about her husband who had recently passed on. I then psychically heard a man's voice reading me lines from affectionate love letters, though I could not see him physically or even psychically. I spoke some of these lines to the woman, who started to weep. I discovered that they were private lines which he had composed for letters he had written to her whilst he was alive. I could not possibly have known the affectionate terms of endearment and other phrases which were special to these two people. This encounter helped her in several ways. It turned out that he had been a titled gentleman of some renown who had left a highly complex last will and testament, and through this psychic contact he was able to throw some light on his real wishes regarding the settlement of his affairs. Naturally this did not alter the will in any way, but helped her to understand it. More importantly still, she was able to bring about a greater control over her grief at the bereavement, in the comforting knowledge that, although her beloved husband was no longer physically alive, he still existed somewhere else.

Countless examples like this could be cited by many psychics. It is not necessary to enter any trance condition in order to receive clairaudiently information that can help someone, nor is it necessary to go into any special environment in order to do this. I was in fact seated in the foyer of a large hotel in Switzerland when I talked to this woman and received the psychic information from her late husband. Certainly, in the early stages, to aid the development of psychic hearing it is helpful to have a conducive, pleasant environment with mystical objects of significance to you. But as you start to develop the ability, providing you are in the right mood and the conditions are right for you, you should be able to do this in a variety of environments.

The more advanced the psychic, the more advanced the

reading and the type of psychic contact he or she will receive. This sounds very obvious but it is still a useful yardstick to follow. In other words, if a person who is obviously rather coarse and selfish claims to be in contact with a highly elevated Spiritual Master, you should immediately be suspicious because there would need to be some kind of rapport between the clairaudient and the person communicating with him. It would be possible for a more advanced clairaudient to receive communications under certain conditions from a more basic communicator than him- or herself, but it would not be possible in most cases for an extremely basic clairaudient to receive communications from a highly advanced communicator.

In practising clairaudience I would recommend again the practice of watchfulness beforehand. This will help you to start to observe thoughts as they enter the brain, which acts rather like a radio receiver set. It receives a signal that travels in thought waves of psychic energy rather than in radio waves. Science has made tremendous breakthroughs in studying and analysing sound waves, but it has not grappled so successfully with progress in the psychic sciences.

THE YIN-YANG SYMBOL

To understand this, it is helpful to look back to traditional metaphysical teachings. For example, the Yin-Yang symbol (see opposite), which is thought to go back thousands of years, illustrates among other things part of a sine wave curve. If you were to extend this symbol (as shown in the lower diagram), you would see a complete sine wave curve, which is fully balanced and symmetrical.

There is far more to the Yin-Yang symbol than many realise. It represents the two separate but paradoxically inseparable forces that govern all life—this kind of apparent paradox is typical of ancient Chinese wisdom. It also shows that all life is energy and operates in a wave motion. Just as

The Yin-Yang symbol

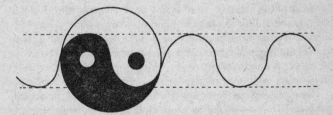

The Yin-Yang symbol extended to show sine wave curve

our brain receives thoughts that travel in a sea of mind energy in wave motion towards us, so it can be used in a different mode, to receive thoughts transmitted deliberately by an outside communicating person. The difference here is in the mood or state of being of the practitioner. We are no longer activating our brain and drawing on certain types of thought, but making our brain receptive and allowing thoughts to enter from a communicating source, who may be on a higher realm or in another physical location. This has been definitely proved through successful demonstrations of telepathy.

TELEPATHY

I am sure you have come across instances where someone has uttered the exact words you were thinking. Phrases such as 'you read my mind' or 'you picked up my thoughts' are commonplace. The practice of telepathy can be learnt, but it is certainly not easy. It is interesting to note that CIA papers released over the last twenty years have shown that tremendous research was done behind the former 'Iron Curtain', and to a lesser extent in the West, into the use of ESP for the purposes of psychic warfare during the Cold War. One of the practices looked at particularly was telepathy because of its advantages in transmitting information without the normal risks of the message being intercepted. Another idea explored was the ability to read the mind of an enemy.

On a far more positive note, it is believed that the ancient communities of advanced men and women referred to as the Great White Brotherhood, located in the Himalayas and other retreats from mass civilisation, have been known to communicate perfectly with one another without the use of the audible voice. In this way the communion is said to be more complete in that there is less need to bother with verbalisation and it is possible to transmit more closely the feeling behind the thought, as well as the words.

Telepathy is difficult to practise not only because of the problem of receiving thoughts, but also because of the difficulty of sending a strong enough thought signal for the telepath to pick up. Clairaudience with a higher psychic plane can be easier because of the rapport which can be achieved so closely between the psychic and the guide, who is able to lock in very closely to the psychic's consciousness and create a strong link. The clairaudient's function is to go from the normally active mental state of drawing on the sea of mind energies to a more passive state in which he allows no interference from his conscious mind. He is alert but, at the same time, passive.

If you wish to practise clairaudience in this way, it is a good thing first to put out a respectful mental request to your guide to communicate with you, and then to wait and see what thoughts emerge in your mind. This request can be done in the form of a prayer if you prefer. In the early stages you will observe a jumble of haphazard thoughts and it will be difficult to discriminate between your own thoughts and those coming from an outside source. This discriminatory ability is in fact the key skill that needs to be developed. Gradually you will start to be able to do this, but it is highly possible that in the early stages mistakes will be made. As with other psychic practices, it is always sensible to keep an open mind and a degree of humility when practising clairaudience.

I must stress here the vast difference between the genuine practice of clairaudience and the danger of hearing imagined voices which can, at worst, lead to a form of schizophrenia. Clairaudience is a controlled practice performed in a balanced state of mind, in which you calmly observe the thoughts entering your consciousness. A schizophrenic condition, on the other hand, is caused by a mental imbalance leading to an uncontrolled imaginative state of consciousness, in which the individual very often invents the type of messages he subconsciously wants to hear. Schizophrenics who claim to hear psychic voices will often obey them unthinkingly and use them as an excuse for their actions, which can be anything from bizarre to criminal. The balanced practitioner of clairaudience will assess the messages logically and only act upon them if he believes that it is wise and correct to do so.

If there is any doubt about the mental balance of a person, he or she should not practise clairaudience. If you think you are hearing voices but are unsure whether they are your imagination or a genuine clairaudient impression, I would advise you to err on the side of caution and not jump to any definite conclusions until they are confirmed through the substance of the messages themselves. A good communicating guide should be able to supply you with information which you could not have known consciously, subconsciously or by imaginative invention. This will be your yardstick for genuine clairaudience.

DISCRIMINATION

There are two main ways to develop the necessary discrimination in clairaudience. Firstly you will learn to recognise that a different vibration is being emitted towards you. You will start to feel the presence of somebody else and be able to tell the difference between your own state of consciousness, which should be as elevated as possible, and another vibration being transmitted to you. Communicating intelligences will usually have their own passwords, particular phrases or signals which you will become used to. It can be as simple as a particular feeling associated with a particular guide.

You will not be in an active mental state in which you are consciously thinking about things, but will be passively receiving whatever thoughts happen to go through the brain. Mystical exercises and yoga practices will help you to learn the sensitivity necessary to develop this skill of discrimination. Because you are not thinking actively about something in this state, you will be an observer of thoughts and there will come a stage when you will also be impressed by outside feelings and vibrations which you know are not coming from yourself. A different type of phraseology of those thoughts, which again you know not to be from yourself, will also come to you, and it is then that you may be receiving guidance from an outside source. I must stress that in the early stages you should keep a very open mind and not jump to any conclusions until you are really sure about them.

The other way to develop this essential discrimination between your own thoughts and outside impressions is the use of psychic hearing. As well as a different vibration and phraseology in an outside communication, you will start to hear psychic sounds with those thoughts. If you were psychically hearing no particular sound but only thoughts emerging in your brain, it would be difficult to know for sure that they were not your own thoughts. Clairaudience will be the critical factor in determining the difference between your own mind and the impressions emitted to you from another mind. Providing you practise patiently, there will come a stage when you will start to hear the distinct characteristics of the voice transmitting the message. This is not a physical sound, it is heard by the inner ear.

As you advance further with this practice you may start to receive words you have never heard before which turn out to have a significant meaning. You may hear phrases in a foreign language which you do not know. This is difficult to do but after practice it can be done. For example, I received a message once while giving a reading to a Belgian and was staggered to learn that the words I received clairaudiently were in fact accurate Flemish, although this is a language I have never learnt.

The ultimate test will be the content of the psychic message received, and that alone can prove its validity completely. For example, if information is received which you could not have known, which was not lodged in your subconscious mind and which proves to be correct, then this is a very good guide to its accuracy. When I first started to practise this, in order to improve my abilities a particular guide who had lived through the Victorian era in Britain gave me information about Charles Dickens' novels, several of which I had not read before. I could then check this information in the various books, which was one way of testing myself for accuracy.

The more you delve into the psychic sciences, the more possibilities emerge and therefore the harder it is to give fool-proof evidence of any particular practice. For example, if you believe in reincarnation, as I do, you may believe you have information locked in your subconscious mind of which you are not aware and mistakenly think you have received a message from an outside source, when in fact you are tapping very deeply buried memories. So you always have to analyse these things carefully. But there will come a stage when you can discriminate through your own psychic feeling and clairaudient ability between your own thoughts and the reception of a message from another person. There is a difference between the state of consciousness you need to enter to obtain inspired clairaudient information—elevated, but passive and receptive—and the state of consciousness you need to enter to generate inspired thoughts of your own—elevated, but active and creative.

The sounds you hear clairaudiently are not physical, but they can sound just as definite as physical sounds. The voice of a communicator can be distinctive to you and even though, as in my case, you may be poor at mimicry, you can virtually speak out loud with the accent of that person when he is impressing you with his thoughts. In such a case, speaking out loud would not involve any trance condition, but would be purely a verbalisation of what you were receiving on a psychic level.

I would recommend that you start to write down any psychic messages you receive, or indeed any other clairaudient experiences you have, because there are many other psychic sounds you can learn to hear, apart from communications from higher realms. Even the function of the psychic centres and the flow of energy through the channels within the aura can be heard by the inner ear, particularly prior to or during elevated mystical states of consciousness.

There is a very big difference between writing down clairaudient messages you receive and the practice of 'automatic writing'. In the first case you are in full control of what you are doing and are consciously aware of the message you receive—you are simply writing it down as a record for later study. In 'automatic writing' the practitioner is generally overshadowed by a psychic entity who does not just impress the mind but also guides the hand. In certain cases this may be a dangerous practice, because the practitioner will tend to enter a negative trance and may, at worst, be possessed by a promiscuous entity. But providing you remain in control and do not practise 'automatic writing', it is a very good thing to keep a written log of your clairaudient experiences.

You will certainly make mistakes in the early stages, but with practice, a sense of humour and above all perseverance, you can gradually develop the sense of psychic hearing. This is one way to unlock those inner attributes that so many neglect and leave untapped, and yet which dwell within the innately divine nature of each of us. How many times have you heard the phrase 'the still small voice within' to describe this divine nature which is expressed through what is tantamount to a high form of clairaudience? It is, in effect, the voice of the inner self.

7
The Inner Self

*

The practice of clairvoyance and clairaudience points to the existence of higher senses within us all, which only need to be awakened and developed. The other three senses—smell, touch and taste—also have a psychic aspect on a higher plane of being.

We have seen an outpouring from the East of knowledge that was formerly kept hidden. One of the most revealing of these publications was an advanced book written by Rama Prasad, *Nature's Finer Forces*,[1] which reveals the innermost secrets of the science of breath (*pranayama*) by publishing a formerly secret Sanskrit text. This science was regarded by the Rishis as the highest of all spiritual practices. The book also describes in detail the meaning of the Sanskrit term *tattva* and the ancient philosophy connected with it.

The *tattvas* are the qualities of existence. There are five *tattvas*, each one being associated with one of the five senses. Rama Prasad attributes far more to them than just the physical attributes with which we are all familiar. He states that all life is permeated by these five qualities and that in the beginning of creation the five *tattvas* imbued all living things and bestowed upon them the characteristics of their manifestation. It is a complex book which illustrates in depth the

point I made in chapter 5, that really there is no sixth sense,
only five higher senses complementary to the five we already
have. In the terminology of Rama Prasad, these would be the
five *tattvas* and each of the physical senses would only be one
basic aspect of them.

CLAIRSENTIENCE

Psychic smells are very much affected by different environments. For example, a fragrance can exist around a saintly or
highly compassionate person even though he or she is not
wearing any perfume or exuding any physical smells. This is
a manifestation of the high vibration the person is emanating,
which a clairsentient person (a person with the ability of psychic smell) can detect. A great healer can also emit a beautiful
psychic smell. On the other hand a very sick person may
radiate a very pungent smell which derives from the vibrations
emitted through his or her illness. A very angry or bitter
person can also emit an unpleasant aroma which has nothing
whatsoever to do with physical cleanliness. Clairsentience acts
as a meter to detect and translate vibrations through this
psychic sense of smell.

Buildings and even districts may emit smells of a psychic
nature denoting the vibrations of the area or the thought patterns and emotions of the people who dwell or have dwelt
there. For example, if one visits an inner city area of violence
and crime, quite apart from the unpleasant toxic fumes often
associated with such areas, there may be an unpleasant psychic smell as well. In a beautiful country district, where some
of the physical smells are attractive and some certainly are
not, the psychic aroma in an unspoiled area of natural beauty
can be as beautiful as the vision of such a country scene itself.
This is because of the emanations or vibrations from nature,
possibly from the animal life existing there, and so on.

Incidentally, it is not just an old wives' tale that nature

spirits, fairies and devic life-forms exist. This is a fascinating subject which has been covered by many writers, including the late Geoffrey Hodson whose book *The Kingdom of the Gods* is a masterpiece on the subject.[2] I was fortunate enough to meet him in New Zealand shortly before his passing and I have no doubt that he was an expert in this and many other occult fields. Benign psychic entities inhabit both country and town districts in order to control the energies and forces that exist there, and it is quite possible to detect their vibrations and emanations through the psychic senses. For example, a walk in the woods alone, when one is filled with spiritual thoughts and possibly engaged in prayer or some other form of mystical practice, can result in a definite response from the local fairies and elves and other devic life-forms. You can feel this love enfold you, even though you may not be able to see them psychically.

On occasions these nature spirits, who are generally happy, especially in a country area which is untarnished by mankind, can be seen and many sightings have been made. They are also sometimes heard to chatter or laugh. One way you can detect their vibrations is by psychically smelling the scent of pleasant psychic aroma, which they often emit in response to any good vibrations sent out by human beings.

PSYCHIC TOUCH

Psychic touch is most directly associated with the giving of Spiritual Healing through the laying on of hands. Large numbers of religious and metaphysical organisations practise Spiritual Healing, though they may give it another name. Spiritual Healing is a very different thing from faith healing in that it is purely the channelling of spiritual energy and does not necessarily have anything to do with faith in a particular religious belief.

A vast array of different approaches and techniques exist,

but they really all boil down to the same basic principle—
spiritual energy is channelled through the palms of the hands
and sometimes the fingers of the healer into the aura of the
patient. Many faith healers would strongly deny this and
would probably even refute the existence of an aura and psychic energy. Nevertheless, they often channel energy, whether
they realise it or not, through themselves into the patient, and
they use the principle of psychic touch to do this. The contact
is made not so much between the healer's physical hands and
the physical body of the patient, but the psychic energy flowing through those hands into the psychic counterpart or aura
of the patient.

Healing is a vast subject about which any number of books
have been written. I would particularly recommend Dr
George King's *You Too Can Heal*,[3] which revolutionised the
healing movement when it was published in 1976 by proclaim-
ing that anyone who has a real desire to do so can learn to
give Spiritual Healing in a safe and effective manner. Happily,
during the 1980s it gradually became the general view of most
Spiritual Healers that anyone can learn to become a healer
and practise this wonderful, balanced form of treatment which
works very well in cooperation with other medical systems. It
is one of the best ways for developing psychics to learn to
control the psychic energies flowing through them, by con-
ditioning these energies with their love for the sick person. If
you choose to do this, it will release the latent abilities within
you in a gradual, balanced and safe manner. It is an excellent
thing to practise in addition to other development exercises,
meditations and so on. Generally you will find, I am sure,
that by incorporating into your programme of personal development ways of helping and serving others, it will be far more
effective not only for them but also for yourself.

If you decide to practise Spiritual Healing you will start to
feel psychic energy passing through the palms of your hands.
This may feel like heat in the palms. You may also experience

a feeling rather like a cold chill running from the top of the head through you as the spiritual energy enters your aura before being channelled into the patient. As you progress in Spiritual Healing your sense of psychic touch will develop further and you may start to feel the aura of the patients when you give your treatments. This in itself can be very useful because it enables you to ensure that the aura is harmonised. By touching the aura you will be able to detect, if you develop the ability of psychic touch sufficiently, those areas where the aura may be imbalanced and is therefore in need of treatment. Such treatment not only helps the aura but has a direct, beneficial reflection on the physical body of the patient as well, even though you are working essentially on a psychic as opposed to a physical level.

Some faith healers would object to this analysis and say it is all a question of accepting Jesus or God into your life. I do not wish to detract in any way from faith in Jesus or God. However, faith is only a starting point to be followed up by action—faith without works is dead. The action in this respect is the transmission of energy through the healer into the patient. Many healers actually go out of their way to avoid requesting any particular faith or belief by the patient and yet their healing results can be extremely effective and, more importantly, lasting, which is not always the case with faith healing.

When giving healing you may also start to pick up a certain amount of information about the patient psychically, through touching him and coming into contact with his aura. If this should start to happen to you, you are then virtually practising psychometry. Should you start to receive accurate psychic information when coming into contact with a person's aura, you are picking up the psychic vibrations of that person and then your brain is translating these vibrations into intelligible information. You can virtually read his state of health, mind or even in some cases his past. Your translating mechanism called the brain interprets this information received through psychic touch. This type of psychic ability is sometimes developed through practising the laying on of hands, although your main motive of course will be to give healing to the patient.

PSYCHIC TASTE

Finally we come to the sense of psychic taste, which is very rarely mentioned and yet exists as surely as any other psychic sense. In certain schools of Raja and Kundalini Yoga, the sense of psychic taste is taken as a hallmark of a degree of advancement. Raja Yoga, as mentioned earlier, is the system which is used to control the mental and psychic abilities of the individual in the overall pursuit of higher wisdom. Kundalini Yoga is a more exclusive and dangerous practice which should only be done under the correct supervision of a genuine Master, since it involves manipulating the highest natural energy within us, known as *kundalini*, which can release the full potential of all our psychic centres through a very rigorous and highly disciplined series of exercises.

It is taught in some mystic schools and *ashrams* that as advancement takes place within the individual, particularly through the practice of certain breathing exercises, a secretion of a psychic fluid from the tongue takes place. This is referred to as ambrosia or the nectar of the gods in ancient Greek mythology and is one of the signs experienced by the individual who is developing an elevated mystical state of consciousness. This particular fluid is said to surpass all other flavours and tastes on earth. It is reputedly an experience far beyond the imaginings of the most inventive gourmet, but, being without the materialistic trappings and vibrations of physical food, goes beyond even that. This type of psychic taste is in fact associated with the highest of vibrations which leads to a state of profound awareness, causing a blissful sensation to enfold the practitioner.

It must be possible to use psychic taste for the purpose of divination, but it would be an extremely rare practice and one I have never come across personally. The very phrase 'it leaves a nasty taste in my mouth' expresses a psychic or intuitive response to an unpleasant situation. All the different senses have different purposes and characteristics, and they bring different forms of knowledge. But clairvoyance and clairaudience have the most immediate relevance to the developing psychic, and are the most commonly gained psychic abilities.

HIGHER CONSCIOUSNESS

Some psychic experiences can lead us beyond normal ESP into something deeper—virtually into contact with a higher aspect of our inner being which could be referred to as the inner self. Many people, after having a psychic experience of one kind or another, have reported a deep sense of spiritual fulfilment or a blissful type of sensation filling them. Not only can psychic development be a very exciting thing, it can also lead to these types of heightened states of consciousness which point to what some would call the divine presence within us all.

A psychic person will tend to become more physically sensitive as well, which is a basic reflection of his or her greater psychic sensitivity. Such development can heighten your normal physical sense of vision, hearing and other senses. For example, a friend of mine was performing a mystical exercise and found that he could physically hear the ash falling from the end of an incense stick at the other end of the room, as though it was a loud crashing sound. It sounds like the description of a drug-enhanced experience, but it certainly was not. He was in a psychically attuned state at that time, which was having an effect upon his physical senses as well.

It is important not to exaggerate this type of thing in your own mind, but at the same time these things do happen to people. Should anything like this happen to you, I would advise you to make a point of keeping your feet firmly on the ground and not taking it too seriously. Gradually you will find that you can gain a control over this type of heightened sensitivity which in certain cases can be a little uncomfortable. On other occasions, though, it can be very useful, especially in the case of enhanced vision and hearing.

One of the best lessons I have come across, regarding the importance of not getting carried away with mystical and psychic experiences, is contained in an excellent book entitled *Autobiography of a Yogi* by the great yogi Yogananda.[4] In one memorable passage he describes how he entered an elevated state which he called cosmic consciousness. This was the greatest state he had ever experienced—it gave him a sense of complete oneness with all living things both on earth and throughout the cosmos. He experienced a feeling of understanding and realisation of the nature of the universe and the purpose of life, which he had never had before. He was in a deeply blissful condition, way beyond the type of ecstasy we associate, for example, with a wonderful sexual experience.

After coming out of this state of consciousness, he went into the presence of his guru, Sri Yukteswar, who had in fact helped him to attain this state by transmitting his own psychic power and mental energy to his disciple. But rather than allowing Yogananda to bask in the glory and dwell in the memory of this experience, thereby losing touch with the mundane reality of ordinary living, the guru immediately gave him a broom and told him to do some sweeping up around his *ashram*. In this incident Sri Yukteswar taught Yogananda and all those of us who have read this story a very valuable lesson. It was important for Yogananda, after such an elevated state of consciousness which had greatly heightened his sensitivity and awareness, to gain a control over it and to bring his feet firmly back down to the ground by performing these menial tasks around the *ashram*.

The same lesson applies to lesser states than the one enjoyed by Yogananda. Very often, after having a psychic experience, rather than basking in it, discussing it at length with friends and tending to lose touch with normal day-to-day living, you should go out of your way to do the exact opposite. Engage in a very down-to-earth task such as washing up or some other essential chore around the house. It would be a good thing to perform some physical exercises, go for a run or a vigorous walk, which will help to bring you back into the physical world and hence maintain a physical and mental control over the metaphysical experience you have just had.

Some deny the existence of an inner self. They say that we are purely a result of chemical interactions in the brain and other parts of our physical anatomy, which cause a so-called personality to exist, and that is all there is. Others would say that we have within us a divine spark which is related to the Creator. Such philosophical ideas are very much a matter of your individual religious belief. Belief in the divinity of all living things is generally considered to be an oriental philosophy associated primarily with Hinduism. However, it is not exclusively an eastern view. You can find it expressed in a variety of mystical schools, including, for example, one known as the 'I Am' movement which is fundamentally Christian in outlook, drawing mainly on the Bible. Belief in the 'I Am Presence' is a view also held in certain mystical Judaic philosophies based on the Biblical reference to the name of the God of Abraham as 'I Am That I Am'. However you interpret it philosophically, you will find that psychic development will tend to lead you towards discovering your inner self.

PERSONAL DEVELOPMENT

Different people choose to develop their psychic abilities for different reasons. In some it is curiosity and a quest for knowledge; in others it is to bring about a greater degree of fulfilment and a release from a sense of psychic frustration they feel at the inability to express their latent ESP. It may be the discovery by a person that she has a natural ability in this direction and she just wants to take it farther and learn more about it and use it, rather than neglect her potential in this area. It may simply be a wish to help other people through using psychic ability.

It is on record that psychics have given effective business advice in the past, one of the most famous cases being the American prophet, Edgar Cayce. In his early years he was often consulted for business advice. But on the whole, psychic abilities work far better in a more altruistic context. The more people realise how effective ESP can be in serving individuals and humanity as a whole, the more it will be used in the modern world.

Curiosity may sound a strange reason for turning to the path of psychic development, but it can be one of the best. After all, curiosity has led some of our scientists to make the most important breakthroughs in history. Simple curiosity can lead to a far greater awareness of our potential and the realisation of what we can achieve. Then it often turns into something more than curiosity, namely ability really to help others in one way or another.

But there has always been another motive for psychic development which has touched many different cultures. That is to regard it as part of something greater, as virtually part of a path towards deeper experience. When you consider the inner self and the nature of your inner being, you are starting to take a more profound approach to psychic development. It is not necessary to have this approach in order to make the fascinating journey of personal development, but it would be remiss of me to leave out of this book the deeper views some hold about the role psychic awareness plays in the overall scheme of their personal evolution.

I have referred briefly to the practice of Kundalini Yoga and it is in this science that the most advanced concepts of psychic development are found. This force, *kundalini*, was symbolically depicted in the East as a serpent. This image has also been found in many other cultures, including the Biblical story of Adam and Eve. Within all of us, say the yogis, there is a female power called *kundalini* which, when activated, brings higher states of consciousness. They claim that without this force being activated at least partially, we would be incapable of thought and action. They describe it as being located normally at the base of the spine, and as we advance, whether we realise it or not, it begins to rise up the spine and enter each of the major psychic centres or *chakras* in the aura (as shown in the diagram opposite). When we focus our mind on psychic development and start to tap into the superconscious mind, this force starts to be awakened and unfolds more and more of our mental and spiritual potential.

In case you are beginning to feel wary of these apparently strange mystical concepts, let me assure you that they have been around in both eastern and western esoteric writings for thousands of years. There is no need to fear the power of *kundalini*, providing careful guidelines are followed and you do not embark upon the dangerous practice of raising it forcibly. It will be a gradual thing, and will happen in a balanced way. It is described as a force that can open up new areas of creativity and awareness. A very revealing insight into the effect of the *kundalini* being activated, almost haphazardly at first, is described by Gopi Krishna in his fascinating book *The Awakening of Kundalini*.

Some believe that many inspired writers, composers, artists and scientists unknowingly awaken this force within them-

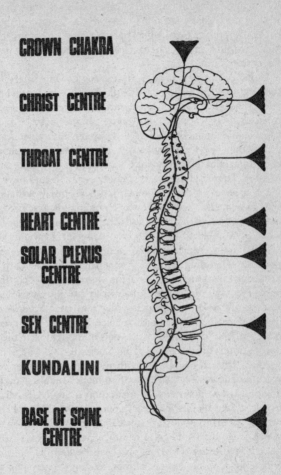

CROWN CHAKRA

CHRIST CENTRE

THROAT CENTRE

HEART CENTRE

SOLAR PLEXUS CENTRE

SEX CENTRE

KUNDALINI

BASE OF SPINE CENTRE

The Kundalini, spine and psychic centres

selves and bring about an elevated state of consciousness
which magnetically attracts to themselves the type of thought
energy which, in turn, when translated by the brain, brings
about inspired music, poetry, scientific formulae or whatever
the case may be.

In the past, teachers of metaphysics who were interested in
the discovery of the inner self realised that a student who was
taking the path towards what might be termed enlightened
consciousness would in one way or another start to become
psychic. The manifestation of this psychic ability would vary,
depending upon the individual. Patanjali's timeless aphorisms
about personal advancement really sum up the whole subject
to a tee. These aphorisms are readily available and have been
the subject of in-depth commentaries by many writers, not
only from the East such as Swami Vivekananda, but also by the
late Christopher Isherwood and other European and American
writers. Patanjali advocated the development of various powers
(siddhis), not so much as a goal in themselves but more for the
purpose of gaining necessary experiences on the path to a
deeper goal—the attainment of the ultimate state of consciousness. This state is variously known as cosmic consciousness,
seedless Samadhi, experiencing the now and several other
descriptions. Whatever words you use, it is generally agreed by
most teachers from different schools of thought that the final
destination is the discovery of the inner self.

Apart from the yoga path, there are several other routes
you can follow, which you may find more suitable. Nowadays
a wide variety of systems of meditation is taught. Meditation
has been used by medical practitioners on the National Health
Service to bring about greater calmness and self-awareness,
which is conducive to good health. The system of Transcen-
dental Meditation (TM) is practised by literally millions of
people for a whole variety of reasons, from controlling stress
to attaining higher states of consciousness.

A very successful Festival for Mind-Body-Spirit was

launched by Graham Wilson in England in 1977. It has since been held every year in London and other parts of the world and has attracted an array of teachers of different approaches to enhanced self-awareness. Even laughter and singing are used by some of these teachers as methods of attaining a higher conscious awareness. Others use visualisation to take the mind beyond its normal horizons through the use of the imagination. Those of you who are interested in pursuing a different path from the yoga-based systems I have recommended in this book would be well advised to attend this Festival, if you can do so. It is normally held in May at the Royal Horticultural Halls in Victoria, but if you are unable to come to London, similar types of event are held in other parts of the world and it is fascinating to see just how many approaches are now being taught to this age-old journey.

Some people are interested in extending their psychic faculties to enhance their life and make it a fuller and more complete expression of their innate potential. Others wish to go beyond this, virtually into a spiritual quest for a deeper realisation within. Either way, psychic development is an essential stepping-stone along the way. It can teach you in a controlled way how to enhance your feeling and sensitivity, to the point where you can gain information which can be of great benefit to others and yourself. But there is a stage beyond this for those who wish to pursue it, which will lead you beyond merely relying on feelings and impressions and towards a deeper knowledge.

Yoga philosophy describes the different stages through which the student can progress in the following way. First, we think about an object; secondly, as we become psychic, we learn to tune in to that object as well as think about it; thirdly, we learn to meditate on that object and then we become one with it; and then fourthly and finally, we enter the ultimate state of consciousness in which we not only become one with the object but with all life. The yogis say we have then touched the inner self not only of the object and ourselves, but of all things. They would describe this as a complete union with God, which is in fact the literal meaning of the word yoga.

In the West, in a more Judaeo-Christian context, psychic development might be seen as a quest for something divine. After all, following an impression or inner prompting is not very far removed from what a Christian might call 'listening to your conscience'. When we start to develop our intuition we do tend to become more conscientious, providing of course we are willing to listen to it. The healing miracles of Lourdes are a very good example of psychic manifestations. Some of the results obtained at Lourdes are absolutely wonderful, but they are not vastly different from healing work performed by spiritualists or New Age practitioners at an event like the Festival for Mind-Body-Spirit in London, or by native American healers or other cultural groups. The essence behind all these demonstrations of healing power is exactly the same, regardless of colour, creed or race. These healings are a manifestation of a psychic ability that is inherent within all people, regardless of the dogma that may be attached to it.

BREATHING EXERCISES

One of the finest methods of personal development is correct breathing. I particularly recommend a very safe, tried and tested system which I have used for many years, devised by Dr George King and described in his book *Contact Your Higher Self Through Yoga*.[5] This gives some very ancient exercises which you can perform regularly without strain or force. They will help you to enhance your mental and psychic abilities in a safe and balanced way. There are dozens of other books on the subject of breathing, including an excellent one by Yogi Ramacharaka, *The Science of Breath*.[6] It is encouraging to note that correct breathing is also recommended by western medical practitioners nowadays, not only for medical purposes but also to enhance one's mental and emotional outlook.

The inbreath is literally 'inspiration' because you are drawing not only oxygen to the physical body but also natural energies into your aura. The outbreath is 'expiration', or a cleansing procedure through which unwanted energies are discharged from the aura. The science of breath has for centuries been revered as the source of all mystical power. There is a great significance to breathing through the left and right nostrils and the difference between these two, but this is the subject of many other books and can be pursued by those who wish to take psychic development a stage further. If you do wish to practise breathing exercises, be sure to use a safe system which has been designed for use in your type of lifestyle. It is not advisable to attempt to practise a very advanced system designed for the easterner to use in a peaceful and relaxed environment in a remote, country or mountain district when you are living in a city under stress with a far from perfect diet!

As well as yogic breathing exercises, there are other breathing awareness techniques you can pursue. Rebirthing, for example, is a very popular technique practised by thousands of people nowadays. Providing it is done carefully, many have claimed great benefits from using this system, which is designed to reawaken the feelings and emotions experienced before and during birth. This, they say, brings a greater sense of self-awareness and knowledge to their lives as a whole.

The Sufis (a mystical branch of the Islamic faith) also practise highly effective breathing systems, some of which can still be obtained. These are said to bring a great sense of fulfilment into your life, as well as enhancing your concentration and spiritual feeling. You may also find breathing exercises connected to various schools of martial arts, where the skills of self-defence are not taught just for practical reasons, but for a deeper mystical one—to gain greater control over your whole being through lightning-like responses and superb physical coordination. Advanced practitioners of the martial arts who use these breathing methods have reported deep states of higher awareness which engulf them at a certain stage in their progress. Such methods are obtainable through the practice of certain systems such as Akido, some schools of Kung Fu and others.

BOUNDARIES OF PSYCHIC ABILITY

We should never use our psychic abilities to intrude on or control other people. When you yourself start to develop psychic abilities you may be tempted to do a psychic assessment of someone who does not wish you to do so. Your motive in this respect may be good in that you are trying to help the person, but you are still interfering with his or her free will and I personally would not advocate this. In my opinion it is wrong to thrust your psychic opinions uninvited upon others or to attempt to intrude into their lives, even though your advice and findings may be accurate and good in every way. Some have found that the misuse of psychic powers has weakened their psychic abilities, and in extreme cases they have lost them altogether.

If you get a strong impression about someone which could be very helpful to him, you may want to ask him whether he wishes you to give your psychic opinion. After all, you have received this information for a purpose and it might be very helpful to him. If you do not listen to the inner self when it speaks, as they say, you will start to lose contact with that inner voice. However, if a person does not wish to hear your opinions and probably does not believe them anyway, I recommend that you leave well alone and do not attempt to interfere. This is not so much a question of social etiquette as the correct use of psychic abilities.

I conducted an experiment one evening purely to see how

accurate my psychic abilities would be when used in a selfish way. I visited a casino and played roulette and attempted to place my bets purely on the basis of psychic promptings. I found that the first bet was completely accurate and I won. The second bet was not so accurate and brought a partial win and a partial loss. The third bet was a complete loss and after that I did not have the psychic ability to win at all. Financially I lost more than I had gained! The key point I learned through this, though, was that my psychic ability was not conducive to selfish motive or personal gain.

Another experiment I conducted with some friends also produced very interesting results. Several of us who had for some time practised dowsing deliberately attempted to use it as a party game. This is a radionic practice using a pendulum on the end of a string, which can be purchased in most occult and New Age shops.[7] After some practice, by observing which direction the pendulum moves—either clockwise or anti-clockwise—you get a 'yes' or 'no' answer to carefully posed questions. The degree of force with which the string moves indicates the strength of that answer. A non-specific movement would be a neutral answer which means that the question cannot be answered as worded or that the answer to it cannot be given as a simple 'yes' or 'no'. Through this device you can start to go beyond the purely conscious mind and tap into your subconscious, and sometimes get a glimpse of intuitive information.

On this occasion, instead of using the pendulum for healing purposes, to help with diet or some other worthwhile purpose, we simply played games with it, such as trying to tell what was hidden behind a screen from a list of choices. Bear in mind that we had all achieved consistently above average accuracy prior to this experiment. For example, in one case two people had gained the same result in a health-related matter when the odds against them doing so were thousands to one. The result of this experiment gave exactly the same message as the casino had done. At first we were accurate, but as we continued the results became less and less accurate until they were not much better than the laws of chance. This again illustrated to me that psychic abilities should always be used for a beneficial or altruistic motive, not purely for personal stimulation or frivolity.

One of the saddest stories I can remember was told to me by a palmist I met. He had given a reading to someone and told him, accurately as it turned out, that he had tried something twice and failed and that this night he would try again and succeed. The palmist later discovered that the subject in question had committed suicide that night and had attempted suicide twice before. I am not implying here that the palmist was responsible for the suicide, but he did feel that he could have done far more to help and that, if anything, he had given encouragement to the subject to go down what turned out to be a fatal path. The result of this was that the palmist completely gave up practising this form of divination.

Had he discussed the matter more fully with the subject to find out what that subject had tried twice, before making his uncannily and tragically accurate prediction, he might have found out about the suicide attempts and, rather than making a prediction, would have given helpful advice encouraging the person not to try a third time in case it proved fatal. He might have recommended some form of help or counselling from a professional source. In my view, he should not have let this case put him off practising completely but it does contain a warning to us all. Always follow your intuitive feelings as well as just making psychic predictions. You will find that when you do become accurate you will be listened to more carefully, and you therefore have to be more careful yourself what you say and what advice you give.

I would not advocate that psychics should follow the principle of the Roman Catholic confessional. From a legal point of view you are not protected if you are told anything in breach of the law by a subject. You may well be legally obliged to report this to the authorities, quite apart from your moral obligation to do so. In the unlikely event that you learn of a criminal activity either being contemplated or already carried out by a subject, you are duty bound to report this, unpleasant as that responsibility may be. Such an occurrence is extremely rare and very unlikely to happen to you, but to be forewarned is to be forearmed. Whenever possible I would encourage a strict code of confidentiality regarding what you are told by a subject, but there may be the unfortunate exception when serious matters are involved.

Certainly, through psychic development you can enhance not only your concentration and psychic ability but, if you do wish to go further than this, you can discover much about your inner self and what it really is. As the mystic would say, you can tread the path from mystery to mastery!

8

The Other Side

*

Through developing your psychic abilities you will gain a much deeper insight into the true facts about life after death. It no longer becomes an issue for mere philosophical discussion when you start to become aware through clairvoyance or clairaudience of those people who have passed on from the physical realm and now exist on higher planes around this world. In my opinion, this alone makes psychic development worth while, never mind all the other benefits which can be gained from it. It is so much more conclusive to receive your information through personal experience than just having to rely on faith or a deeply held religious or philosophical conviction.

You will gain a far greater awareness of the realms that exist around our world. You will also start to perceive the existence of the aura of yourself and others, and those higher bodies which do not die when the physical body dies. As well as psychic perception, there is an even more definite way of determining for sure that life exists beyond the purely physical and that those who have physically died continue to exist on higher psychic planes, and that is through astral projection. But first it is necessary to consider what happens after death.

LIFE AFTER DEATH

The first time you genuinely make contact visually or aurally with a person who would colloquially be described as 'living on the other side', you have come a long way towards solving a vexed question which has dominated civilisations and cultural beliefs throughout history. The term 'on the other side', incidentally, is not quite as banal as it may sound at first. In some ways it is closer to the truth than the concepts provided by orthodox religions which teach, for example, the idea of a heaven above, a hell below and no middle ground for the average person. Psychic information confirms that such people continue to live on other spheres of existence, which are neither heavenly nor hellish.

There are numerous books available on the subject of life after death, which probe more deeply into this fascinating question. I cannot possibly do justice to a full analysis of life after death, but I shall briefly summarise some of the main findings. The metaphysician sees the world as existing in a virtual sea of mind energy. This mind energy is in fact mentally conditioned psychic energy, and it exists not only on the physical sphere of existence but also on higher spheres. Some people refer to these spheres as realms or planes of existence. Others adopt a more scientific approach and refer to them as levels of vibratory frequency. All mind energy vibrates at a certain rate of frequency and it is this rate of frequency which determines the level of existence you inhabit after death. Only the physical body dies; your aura, mind and soul continue to exist on another mento-psychic plane which corresponds to your vibratory sequence.

It is probably from this concept of higher and lower vibrations that the orthodox concept of heaven being above and hell being below derives. But it became steeped in superstition to the point that the medieval thinker actually believed that heaven was just above the clouds and hell was beneath the earth. We may find this a faintly amusing idea nowadays, but it is still believed by some people, who visualise the centre of the earth as a burning chasm or a fiery furnace stoked by demons, and above the clouds an idyllic, peaceful place where grapes are given as food and winged angels fly around. People apparently go to heaven primarily because they have been to church every Sunday when they were on earth. Most of the churchgoers I have met would find such a heaven interminably boring, with no television, no football matches, no restaurants, and so on.

As the Aquarian Age dawns, such superstitious myths as this will disappear. Prayer, healing, charity and so forth will flourish without the need for limiting concepts such as those held on life after death by several major religions. These dogmas will not only be stripped away as a result of new interpretations of the Bible and a re-evaluation of the creed, but by the fruits of definite psychic experience revealing the facts about life after death once and for all.

REINCARNATION

The most important doctrine in relation to life after death is the belief in reincarnation. On the surface this appears to belong exclusively to eastern philosophy, but a closer look at the history of Christianity shows otherwise. It was not until the sixth century, under the sinister influence of the Emperor Justinian and the Empress Theodora, that an ecumenical council of Church elders actually decreed the theory of reincarnation to be a heresy. Until then it had been believed in by certain groups within the Church, including ordained priests and consecrated bishops. The Bible was systematically edited from approximately the third century onwards, culminating in this sixth-century edict, to omit all references to reincarnation.

Many do not realise that reincarnation as a doctrine was

taught during several periods in early Church history before this final edict. The writings of the early Christian theologian Origen, for example, point overtly to a belief in reincarnation. In his major work *De principiis*, which was written in the third century AD, he stated the following:

> Every soul . . . comes into this world strengthened by the victories or weakened by the defeats of its previous life. Its place in this world as a vessel appointed to honour or dishonour is determined by its previous merits or demerits. Its work in this world determines its place in the world which is to follow this.

Here we see an explicit description of what many would call Karma and reincarnation, not written by a Hindu swami or a Buddhist monk but by a great Christian teacher in the early years of this growing faith.

You certainly do not have to believe in reincarnation to practise psychic development, but it is likely that at some stage you will come across this concept either in encounters with those who have passed on from the physical plane and are waiting to be reborn, or in certain cases through your own memory of past lives. In my view, personal experience is the best way to discover the validity of reincarnation. There may come a time in your development when you actually start to remember incidents which have taken place in previous incarnations. You do have to be very careful indeed in discriminating between your imagination and a genuine memory, but sometimes it can be a very definite experience where you vividly remember events pictorially and emotionally. These are often reinforced by experiences in this life which show a recurring pattern, which is meant to help you to learn from an incomplete experience in a former life. The experiences have come back in this life to help you to complete a cycle of experience.

In most cases you will not have such vivid memories, but just possibly fleeting glimpses or vague feelings. You may not be sure whether they are memories or just fantasies caused by historical reading. In this case I would not take them too seriously, but virtually put them on hold and keep an open mind until you have something concrete to go on. It is not necessary to remember past lives to believe in reincarnation, but it can be helpful to those who have developed their discrimination sufficiently to decipher their memories correctly. It is very important at this stage not to talk too freely about these memories to others, because you will find that you lose something very precious by doing so. Some believe that if others are really meant to know about your or their past lives they would do so from their own inner realisation, and that you can throw a person off balance psychologically by giving him information relating to his past lives.

In most cases you will not be absolutely sure of your past life memories. It will be a feeling rather than a question of definite knowledge, and that is another reason why you should not discuss your opinions too loosely with others. If they believe you and you are wrong, it might do them psychological damage to be deluded in this way. It could condition their outlook or their whole lives if their belief is strong enough. People generally fantasise about their past lives as having been heroic or very famous; it is rare to find a person who recalls a mundane life with very little of note attached to it. Those who really do remember are usually wary about talking to others about it because it is so personal to them, and they are living a very different life now. We should not fall into the trap of trying to live out a past life in this one—we should have moved on to new experiences.

Certain branches of Buddhist teaching profess that a soul is reborn intermittently as human, animal, fish or even insect life. Others, including myself, believe that the soul needs to gain a variety of exclusively human experiences, some male and some female, through living different lives, in order to have a full and complete experience of life on earth, before attaining what the Buddhists would call Nirvana, the Christians heaven, and others simply perfection. One of the most concise and informative expositions on this subject is Dr George King's book *Karma and Reincarnation*.[1]

A question that is often asked is: if reincarnation is a fact, why is our memory of past lives so locked up within us that it cannot easily be recalled? One reason given for this is that most of us do not use yoga or some other form of mind enhancement technique to learn to recall such things. This is a very demanding practice, somewhat akin to tapping a higher aspect of mind, in which the practitioner contacts his or her deeper subconscious recesses where past life information is reputedly lodged. Another explanation is that it would not be helpful for a person to have too much memory of her past life because such information might well distract her from the main purpose of this one and tend to make her live in the past too much, instead of learning the essential lessons and gaining the necessary experiences for which she was born this time. Certainly you can see that some people, who have claimed rightly or wrongly to have been a particular person in the past, instead of learning from this information fall into the trap of trying to continue to live through these past experiences instead of moving on.

TIBETAN TEACHING

The Tibetans, possibly more than any other culture, incorporate a practical belief in reincarnation into their everyday life. Even today, despite the Chinese occupation of this peace-loving, highly religious nation, Buddhist monks follow the traditions first brought to this country some twelve hundred years ago by the heroic personage of Guru Padma Sambhava, also known as Guru Rinpoche (literally 'the Precious Guru') and several other names of great reverence. Although many attempts had been made before the eighth century by Buddhist missionaries to enlighten the Tibetan people, who were at that time dominated by powerful practitioners of various kinds of magic, these had been unsuccessful until Guru Padma Sambhava made his historic journey into the Himalayan reaches, and brought Buddhism to Tibet.

Legend recounts how the guru had used his reputed skills in psychic self-defence to overcome the many physical, mental and psychic obstacles which were put in his way as he journeyed to enter the Kingdom of Tibet. Once he did arrive he converted not only the people but also the King to Buddhism. So complete was this conversion that the King agreed to allow Guru Padma Sambhava to be the ruler of the nation rather than himself. It was from this time that Tibet became fundamentally religious in its approach to life, religion and government. It also became a nation in which the existence of those who had physically passed on were believed to be waiting on other realms until such time as they should reincarnate again. They were often believed, and still are in some cases, to be identifiable in their new bodies, so much so that they would sometimes even use the same name they had in their supposed previous life. When considering the whole question of life on 'the other side', we can learn much from the traditions of Tibet.

Guru Padma Sambhava's mission was to teach an approach to Buddhism through which the practitioner could gain a direct realisation of enlightenment. This was known as the *Vajrayana*, literally 'diamond path', because of the scintillating yet penetrating qualities of the teachings he gave, which became known as *terma* (treasures). They were carefully hidden in various ways to protect them from misuse, but at the same time to preserve them for future generations. It was prophesied by him and his disciples that they would be discovered through the centuries by individuals known as *tertons* to whom these truths would be revealed. Some of the discoveries made by *tertons* over the centuries were simply a question of physically finding hidden scrolls and documents, usually placed in caskets and hidden in the rocky regions of Tibet. Other discoveries were psychic in nature and often a result of contact with higher planes of existence. The purpose behind this was to spread these teachings at specific times in history.

Certain *tertons* were believed, and still are in some places, to receive direct thought transmissions from Guru Padma Sambhava himself and then make important revelations about the *Vajrayana*. These thought transmissions were sometimes believed to have been placed in the mind of selected *tertons* before they were reincarnated; then, in their lifetime, under certain conditions and when certain signs and events occurred, these thoughts would be released from the inner recesses of their mind, and they would become teachers. Some of these thought transmissions were believed to have been delivered through what we would call mediumship by the guru from a higher plane of existence or by his disciples, also on a higher plane of existence, to and through the *tertons* on the physical plane. It was believed that these *tertons* were often selected before birth and had agreed to perform this task even though they might not consciously remember this after rebirth.

There is a belief among Tibetans that certain prominent lamas and gurus will reincarnate, always in Tibet it seems, and that through the offices of a medium they can be identified and found. The Dalai Lama's soul, for example, is believed to have reached a Bodhisattvic (perfect) state and he returns time and time again to help other souls on their own journey. Those with a different approach to Karma, which is the Law of action and reaction, would say that this Tibetan idea of reincarnating in the same country and with a similar function for life after life is contrary to a true understanding of the purpose behind Karma. It would deny the soul of a person the wide variety of experiences which are necessary, not only in different lands but different races, sexes and religions, in order to learn the totality of experience on this earth.

There is no doubt that the Tibetans, more than most peoples, have understood the need to cooperate with the process of dying, and their method was laid down in *The Tibetan Book of the Dead*,[2] which is readily available nowadays from bookshops. The published version, although undoubtedly modified by generations of verbal tradition and subsequent translation into the English language, describes some of the rites practised prior to the passing of souls. It teaches that the key time is the period just prior to death and that your state of mind and consciousness at that time are absolutely crucial in determining the realm or plane to which you pass after death. Tibetans also believe that this period prior to passing can have a great bearing on your next incarnation, and for this reason special mantras (holy Sanskrit chants), prayers and other rituals are performed by and around the person who is preparing to die, sometimes for weeks or even months. This, they believe, helps greatly in bringing about a successful transition from the physical plane on to a higher plane of existence.

OTHER CULTURES

Another civilisation which placed a very strong emphasis upon the correct approach to death was the ancient civilisation of Egypt. Like the Tibetans, the Egyptians, centuries before them, had a bible known as the *Egyptian Book of the Dead*.[3] Probably because of the passage of time, this book is generally regarded as being less easy to interpret. Some feel it has been permeated with superstition, probably in the declining phase of a once great civilisation, so that it is hard to discover exactly what the early Egyptians really believed about death. It is clear, however, that there was a belief in reincarnation and in the existence of an astral body, which at the time of death left the physical body and continued to exist.

The Egyptian mummy was originally believed to be a way of preserving power on the physical plane after death by retaining a link between the astral body or soul and the physical body, preserved as a mummy. This, it was believed, would give the person in astral form certain powers on the physical plane through maintaining the link with the mummy and the other objects that were often placed with it in its tomb. At one point it was thought that these mummies would actually be inhabited again in some future life by a reincarnating soul and that there would be some form of physical resurrection, but from a mystical point of view it was the link between the physical plane and the astral or higher planes which was all-important to the early Egyptians.

In contrast to the Tibetans and the Egyptians, there has been a bland disregard of any need for a mystical approach to death in the modern materialistic era, perhaps with the exception of the Catholic idea that if you confess your sins on your deathbed and are forgiven, you stand a good chance of going to heaven. This simplistic idea was and still is a very shallow approach to a profound event and must have left many people shocked to find, after their passing, that despite their confession they did not automatically go to heaven.

With rare exceptions, little guidance is given to people nowadays about how to go about dying. Death, after all, is a tremendous psychological trauma, especially to those who did not believe in life after death and suddenly find themselves continuing to exist. The Tibetan approach was designed to maintain one's consciousness at a certain level of mindfulness so that through the death process one could continue smoothly into a life on the higher realms until rebirth was possible. Ideally the individual would enter enlightenment at the point of death.

Many in the West would probably disagree with such a

philosophy, but there has been little attempt to provide any
alternative suggestions, except a sceptical bravura. A fool-
hardy denial of the possibility of life after death, thereby
shrugging off the need to prepare for one's passing, is no
solution. Nor is the blank submission to the idea that it is
completely beyond our control and therefore we should do
nothing about it. Such an approach is a cop-out from one's
psychic responsibilities to investigate such a vitally important
occurrence as death.

By the same token one could argue that some civilisations
have been too obsessed with death and too intent on maintaining a link with those who are deceased. It is an obsession
which has dominated some cultures and not always to good
effect. If one looks at the origins of primitive religions in
China, South America, the Pacific Islands and other parts of
the world, a form of ancestor worship has been practised in
different ways in these places. This was also common among
ancient Roman and Greek peoples. A variety of rituals has
been followed, either to appease ancestors or to try to invoke
their presence. Food and drink would be prepared for them,
candles and fires would be lit in their honour, sacrifices would
be made and a host of incantations and prayers would be
uttered in order to seek guidance or assistance from them.
Ancestors would be called upon to help with childbirth, crop
cultivation, weather, happiness and even war. The practice
still survives in some form among various cultures around the
world.

There are tribes who do not specifically practise ancestor
worship but are frightened of former inhabitants of the location in which they dwell and make every attempt to appease
deceased 'spirits'. There was one such tribe in Africa, known
as the lizard tribe, whose people were so frightened of deceased
entities that they believed they should crawl around on their
bellies at all times so as to not infuriate the 'spirits'. Laughable
as this may seem, it was tragic for that tribe who spent years

crawling around on their bellies! They believed that to stand up would be an insult because it would be putting themselves on the same level as the deceased entities which dominated, in their minds, their every move. Admittedly that is a very extreme example, but it does illustrate how dangerous an obsession with the departed can become.

OUIJA BOARD

The question of how close the link should be between those on the physical plane and those on the other side is a matter for debate. Before we rush to extol the virtues of the modern civilised world, we should remember that primitive attempts to contact the dead are frequently made in the West today. No self-respecting ancestor worshipper would reduce his or her attempts to contact the dead to the level of a party game— and yet many people in the modern world do just this through, for example, the manufacture and practice of ouija boards.

From personal experience I would strongly warn against the use of the ouija board. It is a device that allows so-called 'spirits' to move an upturned cup or other object to different letters of the alphabet positioned on a board which is laid out on a table around which the players are seated. I remember very clearly a devastating example of just how accurate this can be—to the detriment of the players concerned. A couple who lived above a shop in London played this game for fun one evening. A name was spelt out for them and they found it most amusing—until later. The hauntings which resulted from this game caused the wife, who was not psychic, to hear a name being uttered, and when the husband investigated this name in a local library he found that it belonged to a man who had lived in that part of London approximately four hundred years before and had committed suicide there. Unfortunately the game did not end there. The couple's life was made a complete misery: doors were locked from the inside upon them, horrific voices could be heard and foul physical stenches filled the whole building.

Both these people had been completely sceptical about life after death and had used the ouija board purely for 'fun'. Eventually the wife became so ill that they decided to move from the shop, which was their livelihood. Fortunately they were helped by a few of us who were able to use a ritual of exorcism and move the psychic interference away from the building, but by then months of their lives had been ruined. Although, on most occasions, playing with the ouija board will not lead to this type of happening, it is certainly a warning to those who take these matters too lightly. A complete disbeliever who decides to dabble in psychic and occult matters is treading on highly dangerous ground. There is a very narrow dividing line between frivolity and foolhardiness in this respect.

GHOSTS AND POLTERGEISTS

Ghosts have posed a challenge to researchers for many centuries. There are those who completely dismiss the idea of their existence and many who do not. Some believe that they have had definite experiences of seeing or hearing ghosts in haunted places. Again I would advise people not to treat this subject too lightly—there are tragic cases of priests and others who have not been properly versed and yet have attempted to exorcise these 'lost souls', and not being fully conversant with all the factors involved in a haunting they have come unstuck to their detriment. Ignorance is a risky thing in occult matters, and too much orthodoxy can be dangerous!

In some cases priests have undoubtedly been able to improve the situation, but in one or two tragic incidents they have ended up possessed themselves. When dealing with ghosts or psychic interference it is not so much a question of who is right and who is wrong or who is good and who is bad, but usually of who is the most effective from an occult point of view. Praiseworthy as the faith of some priests may be, they are usually not psychic enough to see or hear fully what they are dealing with and are therefore at a great disadvantage. One should tread very warily when dealing with a malicious and powerful ghost.

The majority of ghosts, however, are neither malicious nor powerful, but ordinary individuals who have died and have remained attached to this physical plane. They are people who should be moving on but in some way have become lost in the transition period. They may have become attached to a particular building such as an old castle, a stately home or abbey. They may be attached to a living person who often cannot see them. This can cause great frustration to the ghost, as well as upset to the person in question who usually does not know what is going on and is frightened by strange noises and happenings. A psychic who is familiar with the correct procedures involved can help, but the outcome will depend ultimately on the ghost's willingness to divorce from its materialistic or emotional earthly attachments and move on. Often ghosts are confused or deluded and in some extreme cases they do not even realise they are dead, but feel lost in what seems to them to be a 'no-man's land'. They can be witnessed by a non-psychic person because they have the ability to manifest at least partially, either visibly or audibly, on the physical plane.

The phenomenon of the poltergeist is another example of a psychic entity being tied to the physical plane. Often they become attached to children, because children are less resistant to outside influences and are mentally weaker. They sometimes influence those who abuse drugs or alcohol, who are in a weakened state and therefore susceptible to psychic interference. A poltergeist may be a deceased person who has not moved on to another plane after death, but has a malicious or mischievous intent. It could well be described as a psychic vandal. Some imaginative horror movie producers try to suggest that poltergeists are elementals with a devious and evil intent. This certainly makes for good horror movies and in certain cases it could happen, but generally behind such manifestations there is a human agency either living on the physical plane or more likely in the astral planes, trying to cause fear and havoc.

POSSESSION

In psychic work one must be wary of the phenomenon of possession. There is a very thin dividing line between serious psychic interference towards an individual and mental illness. Some people suffer from both. Sometimes it starts out as a mental illness which then causes the person to hallucinate or imagine negative psychic happenings and possessions, and later to become prey to such possessions. In other cases a person may start out in a mentally balanced state of mind and practise some of the more dangerous psychic practices such as negative trance through blanking out the mind or using the ouija board, and end up the recipient of psychic interference. This can be compounded by the use of drugs or excessive alcohol. Such psychic interference, if it persists, can lead to mental illness.

A person cannot be possessed unless there is some form of mental weakness within her which can be exploited from the other side. A discarnate entity actually takes her over, usually against her will. An increasingly close collaboration between psychotherapists and psychics on the whole issue of possession is to be welcomed, since there is so much interrelation between psychic interference and mental illness. Some cases, which are diagnosed purely as schizophrenia, might also be related to possession. Similarly, many of those who, despite psychic help, continue to believe they are possessed, may be more in need of some form of psychotherapy or other medical help.

A common habit among those who believe they are possessed is to exaggerate. If they are genuinely possessed, this tendency will often be increased by the possessing entities who try to promote their own self-importance and make out that they are far more sinister than they really are. By and large, a possessing entity is a sad and lost individual who has become a psychic vandal in much the same way that sad and lost individuals become vandals on the physical plane. Such people are trying to prove something to themselves, often to bolster their sense of personal inadequacy—they are certainly not the great evil entities they often try to pretend they are. We should not run away with the idea that all those who suffer from possession are in the hands of the devil. This idea only exaggerates the condition and cooperates with the egotistical fantasies of the possessing entities.

Sometimes a possessing entity has a strong emotional attachment to the person it is possessing, and may even believe it is being helpful. One exorcism I performed illustrates this well. A girl in her early twenties, who showed symptoms of possession, had refused to leave her home for many months, much to the anxiety of her mother who asked me for help. The girl just stayed indoors and did virtually nothing. I discovered psychically that the possessing entity was her deceased father who did not want her to go out in case she met a man whom she might marry. It was literally a case of possession caused by possessiveness. After some guidance and prayer, the case was resolved when the father was given very definite guidance in no uncertain terms, not by me but by my guides on the other realms, to move on. This was not only of benefit to him, but released the girl who then went out again as she had before, and started to lead a normal life.

We must not imagine that all dealings with the other side are negative, or we shall fall into the trap encouraged by horror stories and films, which deliberately dwell for sensational reasons on the horrific aspect of occultism. They give the impression that the occult or psychic is always associated with negativity, danger and fear. This idea may sell films, but it is not true and distorts something which should be used in a positive way.

CHANNELLING

There is a growing fashion for what is called 'UFO channelling'. A number of people, especially in the United States but also in parts of Europe and elsewhere, are claiming to be channels for cosmic intelligences from other planets. I am very wary of those with no metaphysical training or pronounced psychic ability who make such claims. The most outstanding demonstration of this ability I have come across is Dr George King, who has been such a channel for almost forty years, but he practised rigorously advanced forms of yoga for ten years before even claiming such contacts. There may be other genuine cases, but there are certainly also fakes and deluded individuals who make such claims. Careful discrimination of the communications can be very revealing and will help you to sort the wheat from the chaff, as it were.

It is not logical, for example, to believe that a person from the Pleiades or some other far-distant astronomical constellation would make a series of contacts with an individual on Earth psychically, and then use it purely for the regular transmission of very personal information about his private life and the lives of his followers. In a case like this I would be fairly sure that such a person was a fake or was in touch with someone on the other realms whom he wrongly believed to be an interplanetary agent.

The more you look into channelling or mediumship and the whole subject of contacts made with the other side, the more possibilities open up and the less dogmatic you tend to become. For example, it would be quite possible for a person to have a genuine contact with a good guide, and still get the identity of that guide wrong. This happened to me when I was first gaining psychic advice which was very helpful to a number of people. I overestimated my guides and believed them to be far more advanced than they really were. I am still in touch with them today and now know a lot more about their exact nature. When you start down this road, because the whole subject is so exciting and new, there is a tendency among developing psychics to exaggerate and to see things as 'larger than life'.

GUIDES

Some believe that a psychic attracts the guidance of people on the other realms who have known him in a previous incarnation on earth. Sometimes guides are interested primarily in the work you are involved in, if this is humanitarian in nature. For example, exceptional healing work may attract the help of prominent healers on the other realms. Some of these healers will be attracted by the work alone, others may have been involved in working with the healer in a former time. This type of background information will not necessarily be revealed by the communicating guides, and often it does not really matter anyway. The important thing is that they are communicating now and their value should be judged by the importance and merit of the messages they are giving. Often there will be a particular guide who acts as a link person or, in the terminology of the spiritualists, a 'gatekeeper'. This guide virtually makes the arrangements for messages to be given and introduces the various communicators if there are more than one.

If you do start to make contacts with guides and receive information from them, do not fall into the trap of overestimating them. This may sound rather strange advice, but it can be very important. Guides have access to certain knowledge which is withheld from most of us on the physical plane. They may be more clairvoyant and have a generally clearer picture of spiritual things because they are less embroiled in materialism and can see the whole picture, as it were, from the other side. But they can also make mistakes and they should not be leant on or mindlessly obeyed. The average guide should be regarded as a friend who has useful information to give you, which can be helpful and instructive but is not infallible, as some mediums would have you believe.

I would be very wary of information given by anyone, including guides, about your past lives. Those who talk glibly of who you were or who they were in a previous life are highly suspect and can damage the gullible, who may be misled into believing that they were someone either far better or far worse than they really were. This can create ego problems or guilt problems and may lead in turn to a mental imbalance. If in doubt, I would disregard any information given to you about past lives. It is sad to come across those who believe themselves to have been some great figure in history when one look at them tells you that either they were not that person or there has been a tragic decline in their evolution since then!

An open-minded approach to life after death will enhance your appreciation of the here and now, providing you follow the cautious guidelines I have outlined in this chapter. Psychic contacts can be made with guides on the other realms and I am sure that if you decide to pursue clairvoyance and clairaudience in earnest you will experience such contacts. But at the end of the day they are only valuable in relation to living a full and balanced life here on the physical plane. That, after all, is why we are here.

9
The Dream State

*

Among the abundance of different opinions about the true nature of the dream state, there is a tendency for people either to regard dreams as a meaningless ramble of irrelevant mental wanderings, or to read into them a deep meaning or psychological insight which is not always there. In my opinion, a balanced approach to understanding our dreams lies somewhere between these two extremes.

It is impossible to give a dogmatic answer about dreams because, as with so many aspects of psychological and psychic research, every case has to be judged on its own merits. There are several possible explanations for what a dream may be, which will apply at different times. Sometimes a dream may be just a vague wandering of the subconscious mind with no real meaning; sometimes it may have a deep and profound message about our life or even about others' lives, and sometimes it may be an astral experience. Let's try to outline some of these possibilities.

SEX

There is a massive fund of psychological dogma about the dream state, which has grown up in the twentieth century.

This is based on the viewpoint that all dreams stem from the subconscious mind, and that through interpreting them we can understand more about our hidden motives, suppressions and desires. Freud and other innovators in psychology turned to dreams as an essential factor in their diagnosis and treatment of psychological illnesses. They saw dreams as hidden desires expressed in symbolic form. Some were particularly concerned with the sexual connotations of dreams and sex was increasingly seen, and still is by many in the psychiatric profession, as being at the root of all human behaviour.

This obsession with the sex urge colours many writings and lectures on the subject of dreams. While we certainly cannot ignore sexual motivation, we should not consider it the overriding factor. It was understandable in the early 1900s that there should be a reaction against the nineteenth-century hypocrisy which made sex an unmentionable subject. This only encouraged denial and pretence and virtually everyone agrees that it was necessary to bring the subject more openly into the arena of public and medical discussion, as well as psychological investigation. But some now feel that its importance in the human psyche has been exaggerated.

As well as a sex urge we have another more important urge within us all, sometimes deeply buried, but which is nevertheless vitally important to our psychological make-up. This could be loosely described as the soul urge. It represents the spiritual desire within us, which is linked not so much to the subconscious as to the superconscious aspect of our mind. The desire for honourable and noble behaviour and an innate sense of morality, unselfishness and goodness are results of what could be termed the soul urge. This important aspect of mind is hardly referred to by psychologists who are more concerned with the subconscious mind, yet it is potentially the most important driving force within us all.

One of our psychic centres is the sex centre. It is certainly important and governs a number of functions, including the sex drive. It is a major centre of consciousness within our aura, which should not be ignored, and it was wrong of some occultists during the early twentieth century deliberately to misrepresent the truth by not referring to this centre for fear of upsetting the sensibilities of their students. However, by the same token it is wrong to overestimate the importance of this one psychic centre compared to certain higher centres such as the solar plexus centre, the heart centre and higher centres than these. With sexual motivation being so heavily stressed in the media and popular culture, it is important to remind ourselves that this is only one area of personal expression. Many people have found fulfilling lives by being celibate—in fact mystical teachings have taught that there will come a stage for all of us, in one life or another, when we shall no longer require sex. Some would say that such would be a bland, boring and unfulfilling life, but advanced mystics have described states of ecstasy and fulfilment that go far beyond the pleasures which sex can bring.

You may come across differing advice on this subject in relation to personal development and the choice is very much an individual one. The key is to avoid undue suppression but to practise control.

You may come across some practices, such as Kundalini Yoga exercises and other advanced mystical techniques, which are unsafe to practise unless you are not only physically celibate but have a considerable degree of mental control over the sex drive. Physical celibacy does not always indicate a complete control over the sex drive, as can be seen from some of the tragic cases in certain large religious organisations where priests have fallen into devious sexual practices after taking a vow of celibacy. This is sometimes a result of excessive suppression.

As well as an overemphasis on sex, there has been a tremendous underemphasis over the last hundred years or so on the importance of some form of religion. During the cultural changes which took place at the beginning of the twentieth century, there was a necessary re-evaluation of many orthodox concepts. Karl Marx's famous description of religion as the 'opium of the masses' was until recently a major influence on political thought. To understand psychic happenings at a deeper level, as we have to do when analysing dreams, religious values cannot be completely ignored, even though modern thinking rejects the limited dogmas of orthodoxy and embraces the whole mental, psychic and spiritual nature of man.

DREAM INTERPRETATION

Dream interpretation is an ancient practice. We know from the Bible just how highly it was regarded in Egypt at the time of Joseph, and undoubtedly it had been practised for many centuries before that. In order to understand dreams, you need to adopt the approach that every case must be judged on its own merits. Since dreams may fall into several categories, and even combinations of categories, you have to be very careful in assessing the meaning or significance of individual dreams.

In some cases your dreams may reveal to you some of your suppressed desires or subconscious promptings. The subconscious mind, after all, stores the information and experience we receive on a daily basis and only a fraction of this is normally accessible to the conscious mind.

Suppressed emotions should be carefully watched when they come out in the dream state. Just because we may have certain experiences and feel certain inclinations in our dreams does not mean that these are our natural desires. It is possible to develop a phobia based on what you dream about, by jumping to the erroneous conclusion that your dreams are telling you what you really think and feel more clearly than your daily behaviour. We should never be ruled by our dreams, for those who fall into this trap may lose their sense of control over everyday living as a result. Certainly observe your dreams and what they reveal to you, but do not allow them to take on a significance that is greater even than your daily conscious life.

In the psychic interpretation of dreams, probably the most important are those dreams involving a premonition of events to come. Dreams may be indications of our innermost desires to fulfil our destiny in life. They can provide warnings or encouraging signs regarding future events. Rather like divination, the secret with dreams of premonition is the correct interpretation of their meaning. Again, rather like divination, this will vary from person to person and it would be foolish to make a blanket pronouncement, as some attempt to do, of exactly what certain symbols mean. A certain symbol or object appearing in one person's dream may have a very different meaning from the same symbol or object appearing in another person's dream. There are certain universal symbols which have particular associations, but even then, individual interpretation is still essential. Some people have recurring symbols in their dreams which they will gradually be able to understand and interpret in relation to themselves.

Apart from premonitions, dreams may be visionary in a different way. They can be highly illuminating experiences of a spiritual or mystical nature, which manifest while you are asleep. These types of dream may be pleasant or unpleasant and the unpleasant ones, which we may try to put out of our minds, can be just as educational as the pleasant ones. I am not referring here to nightmares, but to visionary dreams with unpleasant connotations. When you have such dreams, whether they are highly elevating and inspiring or, on the contrary, cautionary and filled with an air of foreboding, you should try to apply the same interpretive approach to both categories of dream.

According to the aphorisms of Patanjali, it is a highly

profitable exercise to meditate or contemplate on your dreams. This can reveal the hidden depths of your mind and draw out some aspects of dreams which might otherwise be missed. Without such contemplation you may have a false or incomplete impression from your dreams. For example, you may think you have dreamt about a certain person, yet when you concentrate carefully and try to recall the dream in detail, although that person's name was used in the dream and you believed it was him or her while you were dreaming, in fact it was not that person's face, body or character at all. Such a dream then takes on a very different meaning from your initial impression of it.

A dream which has a significant meaning for you will usually be vivid and recallable in some detail. This is very important because inaccurate details can completely distort your interpretation. A significant dream will probably have had some definite and possibly profound effect on your emotions; very often you will wake up immediately afterwards, even if it is the middle of the night, and remember it fully. It will not be a jumble of incoherent, unconnected events or images, rather like a surrealistic painting, but will normally have a clear and distinct sequence of events which may not be completely normal as far as everyday life is concerned, but will have some logical consistency of their own. With careful thought and intuitive consideration it will be possible to unravel the meaning of such a dream. Sometimes this meaning may seem very clear initially, but deeper contemplation will reveal further aspects that will ensure your interpretation is correct.

Sometimes you may have a dream that has meanings on several levels. For example, Alyson, my wife, once dreamt of a desert region in which mainly ancient Egyptian objets d'art, as well as artefacts from other past cultures, were present. Incidentally, she is by profession an antique dealer and is therefore connected to works of art and ancient artefacts. Certain people she knows came into the dream and reacted in various ways to this desert region, but she herself had a premonition that a calamity was going to strike and urged everyone to leave the area, even though there were extremely valuable artefacts lying there, which were 'up for grabs' as it were. Her dream showed the very revealing reactions of different people to her warning, and then ended.

This dream not only had considerable meaning for her personally, relating to her emotional and professional life, but also turned out to be something of a premonition: the very next day the most devastating earthquake Egypt had seen for decades tragically struck. This was a classic example of both a personal revelation and a global premonition combined into one very revealing dream.

THE ELEMENTS

The elements form the basis of dream interpretation. Contrary to the belief of materialistic thinkers, there are five elements, not four—earth, water, fire, air and ether. The first four are those elements of which all matter is composed; the fifth element, ether, is for the mystic and the psychic the most important of all. It is the element within which all matter and indeed all life exist.

These elements will be familiar to those who have made a study of astrology, which is divided into four categories of signs: earth signs, water signs, fire signs and air signs. Each of these categories has three signs in it. Taurus, Virgo and Capricorn are the earth signs; Pisces, Cancer and Scorpio are the water signs; Aries, Leo and Sagittarius are the fire signs, and Aquarius, Gemini and Libra are the air signs. The Tarot pack is also based upon the elements, with each of the four suits—swords, wands, hearts and pentacles—representing one of the four elements. Again, each of these suits is divided into fourteen cards which are characterised by the element to which they belong, although there are differing views on which element represents which suit. Incidentally, the ordinary pack of playing cards has retained this division into four suits, although with different names—spades, hearts, diamonds and clubs.

In astrology, the fifth element, ether, is manifested through the power of interpretation and the juxtapositions and interactions created by the different planets coming into various signs. Ether is not limited to the physical world but stretches beyond it into the metaphysical. It is an elusive element, much sought after through the ages by mystics. Where there is an apparent physical vacuum, ether is present; where mind energy or healing powers flow through space, they travel through the ethers; where the psychic world exists beyond the material plane, ether contains it. In the Tarot pack, as well as the fifty-six ordinary suit cards, there are twenty-two master cards (the major arkana) which have a particularly powerful influence upon the subject's destiny. This influence represents the presence of ether. In the human being, the aura is composed of what is often termed by occultists 'etheric matter'. Some people even refer to an etheric body rather than using the word 'aura'.

It is very interesting to note that in the Yin-Yang symbol the five elements are present even though, at first glance, they do not appear to be. Four of them are as follows: the Yin, the Yang, the Yin in the Yang and the Yang in the Yin. These are the black and the white colours and the dots of the other colours present in each, which total four altogether. One cannot be dogmatic about which is which, only that there are four elements present in this symbol. However, in addition to these four, there is the totality of the whole symbol which is represented by the circle around it—in other words, the wholeness of the symbols when they are all combined and in which they are all contained. The relevance of the five elements to Yin-Yang philosophy is not always taught to students, but it is an important illustration of the mystical properties of the element of ether which lie at the root of all metaphysics.

These five elements are represented in many ways in our dreams. If, for example, you dream about the sea, it represents, obviously enough, the element of water. Turning again to astrology, we can see that the water signs are associated with emotions, feelings and the psychic or intuitive responses to life. Some psychologists limit their interpretation of water purely to the emotional or even sexual level of expression, but it can be much more than this. The water element often represents a psychic force—indeed some believe that the psychic power of Earth as a planet is contained in the waters which are so prevalent around the globe. These feelings are expressed through the higher and more basic aspects of human nature. Unlike the more simple and astrological interpretations often found in newspaper columns and so forth, water will apply not only to human relationships but to high inspirations and intuitive feelings as well. If we dream about a very rough sea with great turbulence, this would suggest an unsettled emotional period in our lives. If the sea is calm and still, the opposite will apply, and so on.

If the sun appears in our dreams it normally represents the element of fire. It represents much more than this, however, being the source of all energy in our solar system. It even has divine characteristics and associations, representing power, illumination and sometimes life itself. Other representations of the element of fire are again obvious—flames, furnaces, burning objects, and so on.

Earth is represented by anything to do with land, including hills, fields, beaches and even mountains. Each of these may also have other ancillary meanings. Mountains, for example, also represent the peak of achievement, or an objective that is difficult to conquer.

Air is represented by wind, breath, empty spaces and openness in general. Again, breath has other meanings because it can represent the energy of life, or *prana*, which can be harnessed through correct breathing.

If you choose to go into dream interpretation, a study of the meaning and characteristics of the elements is the best starting point. Earth, water, fire and air are well understood and much has been written about their properties in both eastern and western writings. In particular, you can draw upon the information associated with astrology. The fifth element manifests itself through the mystical interpretation you apply to the dream and is also represented in any intuitive, inspirational or psychic feelings experienced by the dreamer either during the dream or afterwards, when he or she described it to you. The feelings experienced by the dreamer need careful analysis and cannot always be taken as an accurate guide to the real meaning of the dream. On the contrary, sometimes the feelings and emotions people experience in dreams are misguided, and one of the purposes of the dream is for them to reflect upon it afterwards and gain a clearer picture of themselves through this reflection.

Once you understand what the elements signify, you will be able to apply this knowledge to your dream interpretation. For example, if the sun is obscured by clouds, this may suggest a loss of drive or impetus—a lack of motivating force. If the sun is rising, it may imply not only a new beginning but the likelihood that the dreamer will be going through a very magnetic, energetic period in the future. If you dream that you are in a tornado or a hurricane and tremendous wind damage is taking place, this may suggest the rigours of a negative thought pattern which may come either from within yourself or from outside. A light breeze on a summer's day would suggest gentle, pleasant light thoughts. A flood or a dream about drowning would suggest a lack of emotional control, or being engulfed in a powerful emotional situation. Very light rain, such as a shower, maybe with a rainbow, would suggest a cleansing and an emotional purification, or a pleasant emotional phase followed by a new beginning represented by the rainbow. If you dreamt about a quicksand or any form of burial, there would be a suggestion of being smothered by the day-to-day practicalities of life, and of being literally bogged down in mundane concerns. Additionally, the burial would obviously suggest some connection with death. On the other hand, a pleasant rolling hill or a beautiful sandy beach on which you are walking would suggest a pleasant liaison with the element earth, symbolising practical attainment and success.

These are rather superficial interpretations, but they illustrate how you might go about gleaning some information from dreams through interpreting the elements and, of course, when they are all put together with the other aspects of the dream they can be very revealing indeed.

HYPNOSIS

The dream state is a form of trance, but one which is in every way necessary to us all. Some people feel that they remember past life experiences through their dreams. For example, they will dream that they are wearing clothing from hundreds of years ago or that they are in a past environment, and then they wake up and assume this was a memory of a past life. It is possible that this is so but, in my view, quite unlikely. It is more likely to be their own feelings about the past and what it represents to them now.

There is no doubt that hypnosis has successfully regressed people into past lives, but that is an entirely different type of trance condition, which is purposefully induced and over which the subject has little or no control. He has in fact put himself in the hands of the hypnotist. This can be dangerous if the hypnotist is unqualified, although hypnosis is practised extensively and successfully for medical purposes. Whether or

not it would be a good thing to practise hypnotic regression
is highly debatable. Some would say that if you are not able
to remember your previous incarnations, then you should not
allow another person to hypnotise you to bring out this
memory.

The subject does not usually remember afterwards what
happened during the hypnotic trance stage. The hypnotist
puts him into trance and guides or instructs him first to recall
earlier periods in his current life, and then attempts to take
him into periods of previous lives. In some cases this may be
very disturbing to the individual. There is no doubt that there
has been extremely convincing evidence produced showing
that people have recalled facts about past lives which they
could not possibly have learnt from books or any other available source. Details have been given in this state which were
not even known to historians until facts emerged later in historical research.

Fundamentally it is a matter of opinion whether hypnosis
should be used in this way, as is the issue of mediumship.
There is no doubt in my mind that basic mediumship proves
the case for life after death. Similarly hypnotic regression, in
my opinion, proves the case for reincarnation. Whether these
two practices should be practised as liberally as they are,
however, is entirely another issue and one about which each
person has to make his or her own decision.

ASTRAL PROJECTION

Another very regular occurrence which takes place during
the dream state is astral travel. There has been an increased
fascination in recent years with 'out of body' experiences. A
large number of witnesses have now testified to dying on the
operating table and returning to the body again. Some of these
people have found the experience a very joyful and uplifting
one and indeed have not wanted to return to the body again.

Typically they describe these experiences as being like entering a pulsating white tunnel of light. Sometimes they are met by comforting figures dressed in white, or they see familiar faces of loving relatives who are already deceased. At some point a decision is made, either by them or spoken to them by someone who has met them, that they should return to the body and they do so by travelling back, usually, through this white illuminated tunnel and into their physical body again. A frequent response to this return to the physical body is one of disappointment that they have to continue in what now seems to them a very basic state after the glorious experience they have just had. Others have felt relieved to have returned and to be back with their friends and family.

The fact that people have often found these experiences to be joyful and something from which, at least for a moment, they did not want to return illustrates just how wonderful the after life can be in certain respects. I am certainly not attempting to encourage the idea that people should want to die. There are, of course, certain extreme cases in which patients are being kept alive and forced to live rather than being allowed to die, but these are rare cases of excruciating pain without relief, or where the patient has lost the conscious faculty completely. There is a major difference between deliberately killing someone and allowing him to pass on naturally to the other realms. Artificially keeping people alive on apparatus, drugs and so forth when they have absolutely no quality of life whatsoever is an issue for moral debate, but if people were more aware of life after death, regardless of their religious persuasions, then certainly this debate would at least be far more informed.

Suicide is a crime against nature and does not lead to a peaceful passing or sojourn after death, according to reports received from the other side. Just as there are higher realms, so there are also lower ones, and these may, according to such reports, be extremely unpleasant. Indeed they can be more unpleasant than some of the most depraved parts of the physical plane of existence. Furthermore, the experience gained here on this physical plane is, according to those who have passed on, the most valuable in terms of gaining experience and achieving the real goals of life and mastering the lessons it brings. Although it can be very uplifting to experience astral projection, which is a free and unrestricted 'out of the body' experience, it is here in this physical world that the most rewarding experiences are generally to be found. Those who die with regrets about what they should or should not have done in life, carry this feeling of remorse with them, and from all accounts this can be the most painful punishment, self-induced as it is, that any of us can undergo. After all, if when you pass on you have regrets, it really is too late to do much about them, at least until you are reborn again.

Astral experience can be one of the most invigorating and elevating of experiences if practised carefully and safely. **I would advise you not to attempt astral projection unless you are fairly advanced in yoga practice.** It would certainly be essential to be proficient in the practice of breathing exercises and have considerable control over the aura, psychic centres and psychic channels within the aura before attempting this consciously. You would also require a considerable degree of willpower and mental discipline.

Astral projection often occurs involuntarily, and this is where the dream state can be confused with an astral experience. Some apparent dreams are, in fact, examples of astral projection to another realm or even another part of this physical realm. In the sleep state an inhibiting part of the consciousness is removed and a form of mental trance is induced. The exact nature of this trance will vary from person to person, but if you are able to remain consciously aware, as you fall asleep you may notice yourself leaving the physical body in your astral body. You will see beneath you the physical body asleep on the bed as you leave. You will float off in your astral body and start to travel. You may go almost immediately to another realm in an apparent flash, or you may travel on this realm for a while before doing so. A higher part of your consciousness will be in control of this state which most people could not consciously induce. Often you will be assisted in your astral travelling by your guides or by others on the other realms. The trance state of sleep prevents interference from your conscious mind, such as shock or disbelief, getting in the way of this projected astral state which is entirely natural to you.

Sometimes astral experiences will occur of which you will have no memory afterwards. You may, for example, travel at night and meet up with friends or associates on the other realms and not remember it the next day. You may have an argument in an astral experience with somebody, which you do not remember, and then wonder why, the next day, you are cold-shouldered by him. You may recognise someone you have never met physically before, and yet she is someone you have actually met in an astral experience. Alternatively, she may be someone you have met in a past life, which is another possible explanation for this recognition. When you take into account occult and metaphysical factors, you gain a much deeper understanding of the experiences that happen to us all on a daily and nightly basis.

Astral experience can be good, bad or indifferent. At its best you can learn a considerable amount, at its worst you may behave in the sleep state in a way you would not normally countenance in daily living. Astral travel is recognisably different from the mental rambling type of dream by its coherence, and it is distinguishable from the visionary type of dream by the often down-to-earth emotions and events experienced. You will usually have more psychic ability in the astral state than you would normally have in the physical body. For example, many people experience flying in their astral bodies, as well as other psychic feats which they could not possibly replicate while in their physical bodies. There are very rare cases in which Masters have demonstrated the ability to fly in their physical bodies, but the astral body and the other realms in general are much freer in all ways for mental and psychic feats of a so-called paranormal nature. Undoubtedly the more control you gain over your dream state the more control you will gain over the waking state, and vice versa. The two are completely interrelated and have a great effect upon one another.

It is certainly worth giving yourself time to analyse the dream state. I shall never forget as a music student learning that the great composer Berlioz, who is one of my favourites, awoke with a full memory of a wonderful piece of music he had been given in a dream. He never committed this to paper due to other pressing material commitments in his life at the time, after which he completely forgot the music. This was a source of regret to him. It seemed to me at the time that we possibly lost a historic piece of music simply because Berlioz had to earn a living in the material world. If this is true it is certainly a lesson to those of us who completely ignore our dream state experiences. On the other hand, we should not overestimate dreams or place them on a pedestal above the waking state. If we ever start to do that it is certainly time to ignore them altogether.

DREAM DELUSIONS

Although I have emphasised the positive cases here, it is also possible to have unpleasant experiences in the dream state. Many have received guidance, help and ideas in astral experiences during sleep, some of which they can remember and some of which are lodged in their subconscious mind. But it is also possible to receive misinformation in the sleep state and to wake with deluded concepts about people or situations through what could be termed psychic interference. You may develop an unfounded dislike for someone as a result of unfortunate dreams or astral experiences which you cannot remember, and you therefore will not know why such an illogical thought or feeling has emerged. Such cases as this are among the pitfalls to be avoided in psychic development. It would be helpful to unearth the memory of such dreams so that you can free yourself from the 'negative baggage' you have unwittingly taken on in the dream state.

There has been a spate of claims, particularly during the 1980s, about UFO abductions. As a firm believer and campaigner on the subject of UFOs, I have looked at some of these with great interest and found that many of them are intermingled with dreams. They have often happened either just before or just after going to sleep. University professors in America have attached great significance to some of these because the subjects have recalled often gruesome or sexually-related events under hypnosis and have successfully undergone lie-detector tests. It occurs to me that it would be helpful when examining these UFO abduction cases to be better versed in astral travel and the dream state in general. One thing which does not seem to have crossed the minds of many of these investigators, who fully believe in these abductions, is that they may be astral experiences happening in this world and perpetrated by entities from this planet in order to cause confusion to the people concerned and indeed to the UFO movement as a whole. This kind of mischievous act is just the kind of thing that some lower entities would definitely enjoy.

Some UFO abduction cases are substantiated under hypnotic regression. But just because two people report a case and both successfully go through a lie-detector test or separately undergo hypnosis and come up with the same experiences, does not necessarily mean that they have had physical meetings with extra-terrestrials on UFOs. In some cases they could have had astral experiences which really did happen and

therefore passed the lie-detector test or the hypnosis, but were
not UFOs or extra-terrestrials at all. It is hard to believe that
evil extra-terrestrials are abducting a small number of people
purely for the purpose of performing some bizarre surgical
operation or committing rape when, according to some claim-
ants, with their technology they could easily invade the planet
as a whole. Undoubtedly some of those who claim to have
experienced UFO abduction are genuine people who fully
believe what they say. Every case has to be judged on its own
merits and all the possibilities, including metaphysical ones,
have to be examined. A deeper understanding of the dream
state would certainly be helpful in this.

DÉJÀ VU

Déjà vu is another phenomenon which can be very interesting
and for which a number of possibilities exist. My university
tutor informed me that the first time he visited Calcutta
he knew certain parts of it before he went there. He could
describe where the streets would lead before he went down
them. Sometimes you can meet a person for the first time and
yet you recognise him—you seem to have seen him before.
Sometimes an event takes place which you feel has happened
to you before. People often wonder what causes such a *déjà vu*
experience, and in my view there could be a number of reasons
for it.

   One explanation could be that it is the result of a dream
in which a strong premonition has taken place. Another could
be that you have had an astral experience which you subconsciously remember, in which you were told by a guide about
an experience to come, so that when it happens it seems
familiar to you. Alternatively, it could be a result of reincarnation, which my tutor certainly believed applied to his
experience. He felt he must have been to Calcutta in a previous life and that was why he knew exactly where the streets

led. The same could be true of meeting a person, since although through their different lives people will change physically and will assume different bodies, their vibrations will tend to continue in a recognisable way, so that you will have some uncanny, almost *déjà vu*-like recall of a person whom you have apparently never met before.

Déjà vu may also be a result of a heightened state of consciousness in which your higher self is virtually guiding you by identifying your destiny as it progresses. You may have prepared for some events even before birth, when you were in a higher state of consciousness and possibly receiving guidance and help on the other realms. As these events work out you experience this feeling of *déjà vu*.

There are those whose psychic abilities manifest in their dreams. Through dreaming they can see coming trends in their life or the lives of others. If this is true of you, I suggest you study your dreams and learn to apply the all-important faculty of intuition to them, just as you would to any other form of divination. Dreams should not be taken too seriously, but nor should they be completely brushed aside. They do, after all, represent a massive proportion of our time.

When one looks closely at dreams and the higher attributes of mind in general, it becomes clear that there is a magic pervading the whole of our life. We can either ignore this magic by focusing purely on a materialistic explanation of all things, or examine it carefully and use it to the benefit of ourselves and, more importantly, of others. If we take it far enough we shall start to discover the magic that exists throughout all life.

10

Magic and Ritual

*

Throughout the ages many people have tried to define the true meaning of the word 'magic', but of all the definitions I have ever come across, none has surpassed the very simple yet all-inclusive definition by His Eminence Dr George King, that magic is 'all thought and all action'. A magic is created in all our lives, in all we think and all we do. In fact, our lives are really the product of our combined thoughts and actions. We can build a powerful, positive magic into them.

Contrary to the view that magical acts are only those that would be described as supernatural or paranormal, metaphysical philosophy has taught that these are just particular types of thought and action, bringing results which a sceptic would consider impossible and yet which happen. Nevertheless all our actions, even the most simple, are to some degree magical in their effect, as are all our thoughts.

VIBRATIONS

The vibrations we generate as a result of our thoughts and emotions affect other people and indeed all living things, and this effect could be described as magical. For example, when two people meet who either dislike or are jealous of one another, nothing may seem to have transpired except polite conversation, and yet there will have been a radiation between them of a destructive thought pattern which creates vibrations. This vibrational thought pattern will affect the energetic connections between the auras of these two people, and that in turn will affect their psychic or psychosomatic health and eventually, to some degree, their physical health. A magical act has taken place although there appears to have been only polite conversation. This is just one example of thousands that take place throughout life.

Phrases like 'the air was thick' or 'you could feel daggers between them' describe a sensing of vibrations which, in this case, are not pleasant. In other cases you have situations which 'gel' because of the harmonious vibrations between people. Gradually, as you become more involved in psychic development, you start to see a much wider picture than just yourself and your own energies. The whole of life is a sea of interconnecting energies conditioned by thoughts and emotions that interact and cause a magical effect which is unspoken and yet is continually going on. There is virtually a psychic current or tide to life, which ebbs and flows and which the psychic person can tune in to.

Ordinary day-to-day actions can have far more effect than might appear. The simple act of shaking hands is based on an ancient magical act in which two people are exchanging their psychic energies through the psychic centres in the palms of the hands—the same psychic centres, incidentally, that are used for Spiritual Healing, when energy is channelled through the laying on of hands. This interchange through shaking hands brings about a certain bonding between two people, even though the vast majority of those who perform this simple greeting have no idea that a magical act has taken place.

If we look to the East we see that two hands clasped together in front of the heart centre, which is situated in the aura opposite the breastbone, followed by a bow, is a traditional

Indian greeting. Again this simple act has a magical meaning roughly as follows: 'I am now holding my vibrations within myself by joining the palms of my hands together out of respect for you whom I am now meeting.' It represents the fact that the person bowing is humble enough to realise that the other person does not need his energies and therefore as he greets them he will hold them within himself. There is a magical significance to the fact that the hands are placed in front of the heart centre, preventing the outward flow of energy from this centre as well as from the palms of the hands.

These and hundreds of other examples show that, even in ordinary everyday life, simple magical acts are performed. My grandfather, who knew nothing of psychic things, used to place his bowler hat over his stomach when he was in the company of upsetting people. On the face of it this seems an absurdly superstitious thing to do, and yet on closer examination it is entirely logical. By holding the energies within the solar plexus centre, which is the psychic centre particularly responsible for receiving and discharging energies, he protected himself from the vibrations of unpleasant people. Indeed, when you are in the company of those radiating negative energies through anger, jealousy and so on, it is a sensible thing to protect your solar plexus centre. This is a simple magical act, completely unknown to my grandfather who probably did not believe in magic at all.

RITUAL

As well as these specific examples, there is an effect from every single action we perform or thought we think, not only on the surface but at a deeper level as well. There are also those actions and thoughts which have what would be termed paranormal results. Such magical events can vary from the marvellous to the despicable. They are usually the product of one form of ritual or another.

The Oxford Dictionary definition of a ritual is 'a prescribed order of performing rites'—and a rite is 'a religious or solemn observance'. This type of action is usually seen in a religious context but the truth is that when we examine magical ritual we are looking at something that is little understood by orthodox thinkers. I see magic and ritual not so much as a religious expression but as a natural part of all our lives. It cannot be ignored in a proper study of psychic development.

If you decide to practise a chosen system of divination such as the Tarot or the I Ching, you will find a ritualistic aspect to your practice starting to develop. For example, with the Tarot there is a prescribed order of procedure which is followed with every subject, which is tantamount to a ritual. After a while the very act of following this procedure starts to invoke a certain atmosphere or energy. This atmosphere is conducive to reading the signs of the subject's destiny, partly because you have altered your state of consciousness into a deeper, more intuitive one, but also because a certain magic has been created by the procedure you have followed. The same is true of the I Ching.

One of the key aspects to all magical ritual is repetition. A ritual is generally an exactly repeated series of actions and words which generate a certain magical power. This sort of repetition applies not only to psychic things but also to very common everyday events. For example, if you wish to exercise physically, it is most effective to follow a regular programme of exercises. This may include not only the choice of exercises you perform, but also the time you perform them, the clothes you wear, the people you exercise with and so on. These exercises may be chosen for their aerobic or physical value, but if you develop a routine you will find it easier to go from one exercise to another because of the pattern or ritual that develops.

Exactly the same principle applies to the practice of mystical exercises. It was often taught that a certain set of practices

should be followed at dawn, another at noon, another at sunset
and so forth. There were good metaphysical reasons for this,
concerned with the flow of certain natural energies (*pranas*) in
relation to the sun at these times, based on the fact that all
energy within the solar system comes from the sun. But in
addition it was well known that through making a ritual of
these practices it would be easier to maintain the discipline
necessary to continue with them over a lengthy period, which
might be many years in some cases. It was also known that,
through the pattern or ritual that emerged, a certain power
would be gained by the practitioner, and that even when the
exercises became tedious or boring and practising them
required an effort of will, he would be empowered to continue
because of the ritual that had developed. The practitioner had
maintained the necessary discipline through following a ritual,
which had started to create a certain magic in his life, and
that in turn gave him greater power on his chosen path.

Some yogis, mystics and white magicians would select particular garments in which to perform certain types of practice.
These might include a robe of a certain colour, such as the
traditional ochre robe or another garment which would take
on a particular meaning for ritualistic purposes. This practice
is also followed in the traditional Church, where an arch-
bishop or bishop will wear ecclesiastical vestments of a particular colour at certain times. For example, they will wear
one colour for Easter, another for Christmas, another for Lent
and so forth. There are many reasons for this, some of which
will appertain to the Gospels and the significance of certain
events in the religious calendar. But in addition to this, the
person who reserves certain garments for ritualistic use will
give a certain power to those garments. The magical power,
which has virtually been channelled into them, both meta-
phorically and metaphysically, will have a psychic effect on
the practitioner and will in turn generate a certain power to
the events for which they are used.

This does not only apply to garments—it applies also to places. Certain caves, mountains, lakes or other districts would have a particular metaphysical or mystical significance and pilgrimages to those places would be rewarded with certain magical happenings. This is because the ritualistic use of those places for certain practices gave them this power. This can also be true of certain rooms or buildings. It is not only that the rooms or buildings themselves have a magical power, but the fact that they have been ritualistically used by large numbers of people for many years for that purpose and with that thought and action in mind. You will discover a similar effect if you always give a reading in the same place or wear clothing exclusively reserved for readings.

Peoples from all over the world cherish their national customs very dearly. Some of them have no apparent logical foundation in today's world and yet they are virtually revered. The ceremony of the opening of the Houses of Parliament in Great Britain, for example, is considered by some to be mere foolish pageantry. And yet the majority of British people still want this and other traditional ceremonies to be retained. Usually they cannot explain why, but they just feel that it is a good thing. If you look closely at events like these, including the historical traditions of the City of London and other parts of Britain and Europe, you can see that these events are often full of mystical symbology, which has been practised for many generations. It has become a ritual and this ritual has developed a certain magical power which renders to the opening of Parliament or any other occasion a greater sense of solemnity, majesty and purpose. In the light of the behaviour of certain British Members of Parliament and the generally raucous, rude conduct that can be witnessed on television, the more solemnity, majesty and purpose that can be given to it through such a ritual as this, the better. Because the ritual of the opening of the Houses of Parliament has been performed in a very similar way for centuries, it has gained a magical power which can be felt if one is present at such an event. This power adds something to Parliament and the nation as a whole—though not as much as it would do if it had been correctly devised according to mystical law from a magical point of view.

The same is certainly true of ecclesiastical ritual in the Christian Church. In his excellent book *The Science of the Sacraments*, C. W. Leadbeater,[1] who was himself a clairvoyant and mystic, analysed the psychic effect of various ecclesiastical ceremonies in the Catholic Church. He himself was a Bishop in the Liberal Catholic Church, but much of his analysis applies to all branches of Christian orthodoxy. It is an extraordinary thing that many people who attend church regularly, including many ordained people, have little idea of the magical effects of the rituals they are performing. Leadbeater analysed not only the energetic power that is invoked in the ritual of the Holy Eucharist, for example, but also the mystical properties of the garments used and the way that psychic energies are channelled through them during the various rituals performed in churches. It is an extremely interesting work which would be a useful study for all in the Christian ministry.

In many ways the psychic practitioner is a futuristic person looking forward to a time of change when the metaphysical sciences will be integrated into the fabric of world society. But the psychic person can also appreciate very deeply the value of those traditions that add colour and power to everyday materialistic life. A mystical thinker will very often be attracted by these traditions and will not necessarily be a political revolutionary, although he or she will often be a spiritual revolutionary.

ETHER

Magicians have always recognised the existence of the fifth element, ether. The early Hindu Vedic texts, the *Upanishads*, venerated this as the most sacred and important of all the elements because all the others are contained within it. It is crucial to the magician because this element is not limited to the purely physical plane of existence. Some find it hard to distinguish between ether and air and yet on close examination the distinction is very clear. Air is the manifestation of an element in the physical environment. Ether contains air but transcends it on to higher metaphysical realms. It is not limited to any particular physical or chemical constituent: it is all of them and more than that.

It is interesting that parapsychological researchers are increasingly moving away from the theory of relativity and back to quantum physics, which preceded it, in order to understand and define these emerging mystical concepts. Thousands of years ago, mystics and psychics were aware of things that are now starting to permeate materialistic science. The theory of relativity deals with the relationship between energy and mass using the well known theorem that $e = mc^2$, where e is energy, m is mass and c is a constant. Quantum physics deals with the relationship between energy and frequency, using the formula $e = fp$, where e is energy, f is frequency and p is a constant. It is the relationship between energy and frequency rather than energy and mass which, in the view of most parapsychologists, holds the key to understanding the psychic sciences.

This type of knowledge is found not only in recent parapsychological studies but was also very well known in ancient Indian and Chinese philosophies and indeed in the western magical schools and their quests for the Holy Grail, the Philosopher's Stone and the formulae for alchemy. Indian yoga philosophy recognised that the secret behind all magic was understanding two things: the function of the elements and the operation of the *pranas* which are the energies of life. These energies or *pranas* are the subject of many excellent treatises. The best way to contact these forces or *pranas* was and still is through correct breathing exercises. When we inhale and exhale air, we also inhale and exhale *pranas*, not so much into our physical body but into our auras.

There are five major *pranas* and five minor *pranas*, just as there are five elements and indeed five senses. These senses are associated with the five qualities (*tattvas*), each of which is linked to one or other of the five elements. It is for this reason that the pentagram, which has been much associated with 'black' magic, is a five-pointed star. In actual fact it should not be used for 'black' magic at all, but in its true essence is an extremely positive white magic symbol.

A tradition of genuine, pure white magic runs through western history. Pythagoras was reputed to uphold strict secrecy specifically to avoid his magical practices being misused. For example, he is said to have instructed his students to leave no creases in their bed sheets when rising in the morning, to avoid magical opponents using the body shape left in the bed as part of a negative magical ritual against them. He warned against leaving hairs or finger-nails lying around because these could also be used magically against them. He was certainly under attack from many opponents at the time, and it is interesting to note how meticulous he was about protecting himself and his students from all forms of magical interference.

It is highly probable that there was both an exoteric and an esoteric school of Greek philosophy, both during Pythagoras' time and later. By and large, we are only aware of the teachings committed to writing in the exoteric school. In the West there has always been the existence of these two traditions of exotericism and esotericism. This is also believed by some to be true of the Christian Church which has always preserved an inner core of mystical knowledge that has not necessarily been revealed to the populace at large.

THE HOLY GRAIL

The Holy Grail has been an obsession among western magicians for generations, possibly misguidedly so at times. Immersed in Arthurian legend and the epic mythology so venerated by Wagner, most people have seen the Holy Grail as a sacred relic. But there is an entirely opposite school of thought which I personally find extremely convincing. This sees the Holy Grail, which was reputedly the chalice used by Jesus Christ at the Last Supper, not so much as a positive symbol as something which was connected with a foul and evil act, namely the crucifixion. This and all the other artefacts associated with the crucifixion are, in the view of some mystics, negative mystical objects rather than positive ones. Those who believe this see the quest of King Arthur and his Knights to find the Holy Grail and other artefacts as a desire spiritually to transmute the evil which surrounded the tragic event of the crucifixion.

Even though, arguably, anyone with a true faith in Jesus would believe that He was in control of the events leading up to His death, those objects associated with the crucifixion still have negative associations and powers. The quest for the Holy Grail, from this perspective, was a desire to prevent these objects from wielding this negative power which expressed the magic not so much of Jesus Himself, as of those evil plotters behind His apparent death.

Whichever school of thought you follow, and there are many when it comes to the Holy Grail, one principle is constant to all views: these objects had a great magical power. It is interesting to note that, according to some reports, both Hitler and Napoleon made one of their first priorities on assuming power to obtain the so-called spear of destiny, which reputedly was the spear that pierced the side of Jesus on the cross. They were said to believe that by obtaining this spear they would gain a magical power that would assist them greatly in their evil plans of dictatorship and military conquest.

One of the most interesting legends of the Holy Grail is that Sir Galahad, who became Priest of the Holy Grail when he and Sir Percival had finally obtained it, took it to a place of worship. Galahad was then seen to ascend into the sky with the Grail which was symbolically removed from the surface of this planet in a transmuting flash of light. If it has any truth in it, this certainly represents the transmutation of a negative artefact to allow the real spirituality of Christianity to flourish without the shackles of the foul plot which brought about the crucifixion. Although Jesus rose from the dead, nevertheless the crucifixion had a certain magic which has permeated the religion for many centuries with negative effects. Some believe this magic was a contributing factor, for example, to the period of the Inquisition and other deplorable chapters in Christian history.

Objects do contain a magical power, as can be demonstrated by the practice of psychometry. This power is an energy, conditioned by certain thoughts and feelings, which is contained not in the physical aspect of these objects so much as the etheric aspect of them. Between the gaps in the molecules, which science tells us are massive by comparison with actual mass, are energies of a psychic nature. In the case of a very powerful magical object, these energies may affect all those who come into contact with them. Not only do human beings have an aura or etheric counterpart, so do all physical objects as well. This is another illustration of the way that all life is magical in essence.

ALCHEMY

Alchemy has mistakenly been regarded as purely the desire to turn stone into gold. Some have therefore seen it as an act governed by the financial profit motive, which is to miss the point entirely. The real purpose of alchemy was to gain control over the element of ether to such an extent that through controlling and manipulating it, the alchemist could alter the constituent molecular and atomic structure of a physical object such as a stone and turn it into gold. What affects the etheric structure of an object, as with a person, must reflect on the physical plane. Gold was regarded as having higher magical properties and therefore vibrating on a higher level than stone, and it was this control over ether that attracted the genuine alchemists rather than the desire for wealth, which they could probably gain in other ways. Those who tried to get in on the act for the wrong motives misunderstood its entire point.

Probably the greatest alchemist in western history was the Comte de Saint Germain, who was recorded in French history as having lived for hundreds of years. He was seen at the courts of Louis XIV, XV and XVI without appearing to have aged at all. On one occasion Louis XV was said to have asked him for training in the science of alchemy. In order to avoid making himself subservient, he reputedly offered the Comte a considerable boon in the form of a magnificent chateau in return for teaching him. The Comte was said to have refused this offer, but instead returned the compliment by bringing into manifestation several highly valuable diamonds which he gave the King as a gift. Of course the accuracy of this particular story is open to speculation, but the principle is that through alchemy and control over the etheric energies, one can gain control over physical matter to the extent of materialising objects. Numerous cases, mainly from the eastern part of the world, substantiate this. Even today there are those who gain tremendous publicity out of manifesting material objects through the use of magic. Whether this is commendable or not, and whether it is a correct use of their magical abilities, is an ethical matter and depends on each case in question, but there is no doubt that these things have been and still are being demonstrated to hundreds of witnesses.

THE PHILOSOPHER'S STONE

The Philosopher's Stone is another western mystical pursuit which has been wrapped in mystery, as has so much in the world of magic. It was believed that knowledge could be placed in a stone with certain properties for the person who had 'the eye to see'. The principle behind this was one of advanced psychometry. Certain thoughts and feelings would be placed in a physical stone which would then contain great wisdom above and beyond that which could be entrusted to the written word. The knowledge would be so deep that it would deny mere words to convey it to another, because it could really only be conveyed through feeling—hence the idea of storing it in the Philosopher's Stone.

In addition to the quest for the actual thoughts and feelings contained in the energies in the Philosopher's Stone was the desire to understand the magical procedures involved in performing such a ritual. This science is known nowadays as radionics, the science of the manipulation of psychic energies. Advanced magical techniques would be used both to store the knowledge and subsequently to release it only to the right people when they came along. This is a highly advanced metaphysical practice which is now the source of much study and speculation. Many people believe it will be the main science of the New Age, and it is also believed to be the science practised by the male and female Masters of Earth known as the Great White Brotherhood.

The principles behind the Philosopher's Stone have definite parallels with King Arthur's Excalibur. In this symbolic story, a sword could not be pulled from the stone by anyone other than Arthur himself. But it was a test not so much of sheer brute physical strength as of wisdom and advancement—to be able to draw forth from this stone, symbolically, a sword which, as the symbol of Truth, he would wield in the land of Britain at that time.

All events, and the psychic energies associated with them, have a certain magical power. Some of these have a profound effect for many centuries, and some have a minuscule effect lasting a matter of seconds or minutes, but either way it is important for the developing psychic to note that his journey will lead him to uncover the 'footprints in the sand' which have been left by events and happenings sometimes from centuries earlier, and have left their mark upon the world. They are the signs that destiny leaves in life's pattern. Psychic practices, to a greater or lesser extent, are rituals designed to control and harness natural energies. Through them you can give power and direction to your life and that of others too—some of whom you will meet and some of whom you will never meet.

Our thoughts and actions leave their imprint upon the mysterious sea of mind around this world which is described in Indian writings as the Akashic Records. *Akasha* is the Sanskrit term for ether and it is believed that in *akasha* or ether a record of all actions is inscribed. At a stage well beyond average psychic development, but one which will come to all of us who seek it earnestly enough according to ancient teaching, we will be able to read these Akashic Records and thereby see, far more accurately and completely than any history book reveals, exactly what has transpired in the history of our planet. This, in some ways, is the ultimate in magical rituals. It is certainly the ultimate way of reading the signs of destiny that are all around us.

I I

Signs of Destiny

*

Psychic development is completely natural and transcends all barriers of colour, class or creed. The same basic procedures are practised by tribesmen in remote communities and in spiritualist meetings in London or New York. The principles and methods, although they may have certain different features, names and explanations, are the same. They form a stepping stone for all who wish to cross the bridge that straddles the chasm between basic conscious awareness and intuitive realisation.

ESP IN TODAY'S WORLD

Visions are witnessed, psychic voices are heard, telepathy is experienced and other happenings, which would be described as paranormal, occur to people from all walks of life. In fact there is nothing paranormal about them, they are entirely normal. Psychic events have occurred throughout history, and in many civilisations they have been integrally built into their cultures, whether people have consulted the Oracle, had their astrological chart interpreted by a seer, studied the runes or just listened to the prophets. So caught up is modern materialism in sensationalism and massive promotional political and show business campaigns that ESP and divination are treated much like everything else: as a stimulating game.

The reluctance to take ESP seriously in public (although most people do in private) is partly the fault of teachers in the past. Although astounding psychic feats have been performed by yogis, mystics and white magicians, there has been a tendency to keep these things secret. If they have become known there has been a tremendous reluctance to share too freely the knowledge behind these displays of psychic ability.

This was partly due to a justifiable caution. Undoubtedly there are many who would have wanted to misuse such abilities, and indeed have attempted to do so throughout history, for the purpose of wealth accumulation, political power, sexual conquest or some other selfish motive. But in my opinion the whole emphasis was far too introspective and secretive.

Times change even though the essence of the teaching remains the same. Today the hallmark of the psychic practitioner is expression, not introspection. Rather than seeking to find inner peace, bliss and personal realisation, the emphasis now is upon helping others through divination, healing, teaching and through sharing these psychic experiences. Personal advancement is a wonderful thing and in every way a noble aim, providing it is not done at the expense of service to others. Or to adapt a more well-known saying, 'we are our brother's keeper' in these days.

If you approach your development without preconditions or prejudice, it can be truly rewarding for you. It is summed up by the example of the empty vessel and the full vessel. A full vessel is impossible to fill. Any water or other liquid that you pour into it flows over the sides because the vessel is already full. With an empty vessel, however, the liquid will fill it and stay within it until such time as you choose to empty it again. The same is true of psychic development. Those who have a truly open mind, free of bigotry, fear and self-righteousness, are the empty vessels. They are ready to learn from events *as* they happen rather than having a preconceived idea of what the events will be like *before* they happen.

DEVELOPING PSYCHIC ABILITY

Psychic development teaches us many things about ourselves and the immense, almost dormant, potential that lies within us all. Literally hundreds of people, from all walks of life, have told me of experiences of a psychic nature that they have had. They wish to understand these things although they rarely take the time to do so. But how many people's lives have been too busy to do things they really wanted to do? If you have the desire to unfold your latent psychic potential, do not miss the opportunity in this life. Having received messages from some of those who have passed on and who regret missing the opportunities they had while they were on the physical plane, I urge you to spare the time from things which really may not be as important as they sometimes appear. Allow yourself the opportunity to concentrate, at least to some extent, on your own personal development.

Sometimes this even applies to those who are engaged in charitable and humanitarian causes. It is commendable how some people are willing to sacrifice their own personal advancement for the betterment of others and for some noble cause, but do remember that it can become a habit to deny yourself the space you need even when the opportunities do occur. If you are not careful, you will miss such opportunities. It is a matter, as the yogi, Swami Sivananda, so rightly taught, of not working so hard on projects that your mind becomes fettered and you give yourself no space for your own development. There is always the time available for this, provided we are willing to take it when it comes. If we do not take the time to practise regularly, we cannot really wonder why we have not become psychic.

I have been consulted by people who cannot see why they are not developing more quickly; yet when I ask them whether they are performing certain practices they have been given, which would help them to do this, they say they are not. In most cases, psychic ability is not something that will just fall upon you haphazardly—you will have to work for it. You will have to practise and, at the same time, you will have to keep an open mind. But the result of this effort will be extremely rewarding not only to yourself, but to others as well. The person who always works for other people and allows no time for her own development is not only denying herself something, but all those she helps as well. If she were more psychic, if she had a more highly developed intuition and healing ability, these qualities would greatly help in all the work she is doing for others. They can enhance the whole of one's life.

There are some wonderful books available in occult bookshops. Sadly, they are often highly specialist and very complex to understand. People can be forgiven for not leafing through some of the lengthy tomes of theosophical teaching which poured forth in an inspired surge in the late nineteenth and early twentieth centuries. Perhaps writing in that rather academic and verbose, technical manner helped to make the intellectual establishment at least take them seriously. But as a result they have become increasingly obscure to educated and uneducated readers alike. The hallmark of great teaching on psychic development is in fact simplicity, not complexity.

PHILOSOPHICAL CONCLUSIONS

If any philosophical conclusions can be drawn from the psychic potential of mankind, they are of an extremely general kind. There are two fundamental truths that psychic development has taught me, and both conform with all major religious beliefs, and indeed with noble ideals that could not really be described as religious at all. The first is that the amount of potential we all have is absolutely amazing. Although this sounds obvious on the face of it, the more we start to realise our real inner potential the more amazed we become at what we are really capable of and what we can pick up through our feelings, and start to know and understand. This is not to suggest that we should ever become conceited or self-satisfied—far from it. As Socrates so rightly pointed out, his wisdom rested on the fact that he knew what he did not know. We should never lose sight of our inadequacies and just how much we still have to learn, but gradually we shall start to develop an awareness and an appreciation of our inner potential, and this will give us a certain inner confidence.

As I have tried to stress throughout this book, we should always be humble about psychic development, with a quiet confidence in ourselves, but never an inflated opinion. Although we may develop certain psychic abilities that some others do not yet have, undoubtedly they have abilities we do not have and ultimately we all have the same potential. This unfolding realisation of our inner potential can act as a spur to push us on to even more unfoldment, with a desire to get to the next step in developing our intuition and awakening our higher faculties.

My second finding is the existence of something which could loosely be described as destiny. Although people may refute the idea that there is an overall destiny factor governing life and choose to believe in a completely haphazard existence based on chance, their behaviour would suggest otherwise. It is amazing, for example, just how many people are super-stitious in one way or another. Although they may scoff at superstition they nevertheless will not walk under a ladder, for example.

There is a fascination with the whole subject of chance. Millions of people around the world gamble in one way or another on the premise that it might be their lucky day. I am referring here not just to those who place bets, for the financial markets are also a source of speculation and gambling. Even though people might strongly deny it, a part of them believes that there is a destiny at work in life, and by gambling they are banking on it working in their favour.

After I had been using the crystal ball for some time and had given hundreds of readings with it, I began to realise that you can read almost anything on which you choose to see the signs of destiny imprinted. The only proviso is that you must be in the correct psychic condition when you do it. I suppose the principle behind all systems is really exactly the same, whether it be the runes or reading car number-plates. Throwing coins for the purpose of the I Ching or picking cards for the Tarot are apparently haphazard, but they rest on the same principle that nothing happens by chance. With the Tarot and the I Ching you can make more of a ritual out of it, but it is still based on a pattern of destiny being reflected in procedures apparently based on pure chance.

The ancient Romans and Greeks were particularly expert at reading the signs of life through weather portents and other methods. Indeed, in certain cases major military decisions were heavily influenced by this type of reading, and at one time very few Roman generals would consider going to war without first consulting an oracle or a seer. After practising divination for a while you do start to realise that there is another superhuman factor at work.

THE FORCE OF DESTINY

All these systems conform to this mysterious force of destiny—from this all the predictions and other evaluations are made. It is therefore vital to gain a deeper understanding of what exactly destiny is and how it works out in people's lives.

As a psychic you are able to help others use their forces of destiny that are affecting their lives to the best possible advantage. Just as mind energy travels in wave motions, so

do certain aspects of destiny flow in cycles. There is a good
time to do certain things and a time to be wary of certain
trends, influences and patterns of behaviour. To give one typical example, when the planet Mercury goes retrograde, which
can last for a number of days, you should be wary about
communication. This does not mean to say that you should
under no circumstances lift a telephone, write a letter, give a
speech or communicate important information to others, for
that would be a totally defeatist attitude to destiny. But it
does mean that you should be very careful about your communication and make sure you dot every 'i' and cross every
't' to ensure the message you are trying to convey is fully
understood and received. If, on the other hand, Mercury is
in a benign position in your chart, this would be an ideal
opportunity for you to communicate certain types of information to others and to take advantage of those positive influences. As with Mercury which governs, among other things,
communication, so one can apply the same principle to other
destiny aspects. This is not done in a fatalistic manner, but
in a constructive and helpful way to those you are trying to
guide.

When you receive psychic impressions you may well get
certain times coming to you which are favourable for certain
people to do certain things, or otherwise. Again, this information is given as guidance, not as an unalterable fact. I can
remember a Tarot card reading I gave to a couple, who were
dating, in which the throw of cards could not have been more
positive for their union. Those cards associated with marriage,
partnership and emotional happiness were all positioned in
the right places for a good future together. But I have learnt
from past experiences not to be tempted to tell such people
that they should or will marry. I even refrained from the
temptation to make dogmatic statements about their future
together, which they would have liked to hear. After all, an
important commitment such as marriage, even if it is psychi-

cally favourable and destined to be, will still not work unless the couple in question works hard enough together to make it a success. I was able, however, to give them a very positive and helpful reading.

The late metaphysical author Dr George Hall, who was a wonderful teacher on the science of mind and was himself psychic, was once asked by a man who was contemplating marriage if he would use his pendulum to diagnose the aspects surrounding this wedlock to a particular lady and whether it would be favourable for him to marry. Dr Hall's reply, I feel, expresses exactly the right approach to divination. He flatly refused to do the pendulum diagnosis, saying that if the man had to ask the question in the first place he was certainly not ready to marry the lady!

After giving psychic consultations for a time, you learn to use your psychic abilities in a way that will be helpful to people but will not trespass on their free will. This type of approach will not only be good for your reputation, but more importantly it is a correct metaphysical view of destiny. If you tell people what they will definitely do with their lives you rob them of the opportunity to choose. Lazy people may like to be told what will happen to them and what they will do so that they can be released from the obligation to take responsibility for their actions. Some people, who go from one reader to another, sometimes within days of each other, are only seeking stimulation and want to be told, literally, what to do next. Having been told this, they pick their favourite reading and set about living out the predictions that have been made for them. This is not the purpose of divination at all.

I often feel that the very best way to perform a psychic consultation would be to give only so much at a time. Many people who come to you for advice want to talk about themselves and their lives but do not necessarily want to do anything about them. They are particularly interested, I have found, unless they are metaphysically-inclined people, in their business, emotional and sex lives and are looking to see what pleasant things are in store for them in the future. There is little purpose in giving people psychic advice if they make no attempt whatsoever to follow it. If anything, you may undermine their willpower more than help them if they start to lean on you. I came to the conclusion some time ago that a psychic consultant should only give so much information, let the subject report back to her and, based on his progress and how much he has followed her advice so far, would give them a little more, and so forth. Unfortunately such an approach would be impractical with most people.

Helping people to use the force of destiny to the best poss- ible advantage often involves them in making certain changes. A belief in love and compassion suggests immediately that change is possible and that people can be helped through situations. Certain Hindus, who believe in the Law of Karma, have misused this belief by leaving out the vital importance of love. In certain cases believers in a fatalistic view of Karma have even said that we should not try to help others who are suffering because it is their Karma to do so. If you get destiny this much out of perspective, then you have entirely missed the whole point.

Bad omens, as they used to be called, are there to warn you so that you can avoid a mishap. They are not there to tell you your inevitable tragic fate. It may not always be that you can completely avoid mishap, and there are certain times of negativity in our lives when we have difficult lessons to learn, but you can certainly avoid the worst of them and make the most of the experiences which are, after all, there to teach you. It is a profound aspect of Karma that the more you go out of your way to learn a particular lesson, the less difficult experience you will need. The real value of wise counsel given in the form of psychic consultation is that if you quickly make the necessary changes that certain events are designed to bring about, then not only will you get the greatest advantage out of the situation, but you will remove the need for prolonged painful lessons. This is particularly important when trying to help others who may have a difficult destiny pattern or Karmic period to go through but can still be helped to cope with it. As human beings we are all interconnected, and Karma is there to teach, not to punish.

The old Greek saying 'learn through suffering' became misunderstood by later generations who thought that the ancient Greeks were actually advocating suffering. They were not doing this, but were saying that if you do have a period of suffering to go through, look on the positive side and turn it into a lesson, which is what it was really there for in the first place. This will speed up the experience. Suffering only comes in our destiny when there is no other way to teach us. If we learn the lessons of life, we can make this suffering unnecessary in our lives and help others to do the same.

On the positive side, your destiny might indicate a certain potential which you still have to manifest and take full advantage of. Your psychic awareness will increasingly confirm that there is a superior force at work, governing all our lives. Call it destiny, call it Karma or by any other name, but this, I think is the greatest of all revelations that comes when we start to unfold our psychic potential.

I am very fortunate to have had as my personal teacher His Eminence Dr George King, a Master of Yoga. Some years ago I was staying at his home in California, and was studying a formerly secret Vedic text which is reproduced in translated form in Rama Prasad's *Nature's Finer Forces*. Among the many things this text teaches, it gives a technique by which it is possible to know the three times—past, present and future. To do this, it is necessary to perform a very ancient practice known in short as the 'shadow practice'. This involves a fairly lengthy and intricate series of procedures which have to be followed carefully and correctly, including watching certain shadows formed in the sunlight.

One sunny afternoon, while Dr King went for a rest, the weather conditions were perfect and I decided to perform this practice. I had been doing this for about ten minutes when Dr King got up unexpectedly from his rest and came straight out into the garden where I was standing. He looked at me for about five seconds and then said, 'That's it, boy, keep watching the shadows.' He then returned to his bungalow and continued his afternoon rest.

I had not mentioned to Dr King anything about doing this practice, or even that I was studying this particular book at the time, yet he had known exactly when to come out and give me some helpful encouragement. You might say that he had tuned in perfectly. I must say the practice worked extremely effectively for me that day, and later in the evening I was able to discuss it at some length with my Master who threw considerable light on this book which he himself had studied in depth some forty years earlier, when he was involved in a rigorous programme of yoga practices for the purposes of gaining the enlightened states he subsequently attained.

This type of story is not uncommon among those who have been fortunate enough to study under a Master of Yoga. It does illustrate, though, that as well as psychic attunement there is a force of destiny in all our lives, which helps to guide us towards the greatest possible attainment providing we leave ourselves open.

KARMA

The eastern term *Karma* is now very well-known in the West and is commonly used. It is not just a force of nature, but a precise and definite law about which many millions of words have been written. The essence behind it is very simple: life is a teaching experience and Karma brings us those lessons we deserve and need. If we harm others we shall need to be harmed ourselves in order to learn how wrong this was. If we help others we shall be helped ourselves so that we can progress even farther in our journey of service and advancement. Karma explains many of the apparently inexplicable aspects of life. I have seen archbishops appear on television and admit that they cannot understand how a God of compassion could allow people to be born into starvation, disease and severe poverty. As far as I am concerned, only through a belief in Karma and reincarnation can this and other similar questions be fully answered. If a person has to learn through suffering because of the selfishness or even cruelty of his conduct in a past life, a belief in Karma and reincarnation alone explains why such suffering should be endured from the moment of his next birth.

As you advance spiritually, you start to realise more and more about this force of destiny, not just from a logical or philosophical point of view, but virtually from personal experience. You start to realise, too, that there is a Superior Intelligence in creation, although you may differ over what Its name is—God, Brahma, Allah, the Great White Spirit or any other. Names cannot alter reality.

There is absolutely no substitute for personal experience. According to Shakespeare (or whoever wrote his plays), 'there is a tide in the affairs of men, which, taken at the flood, leads on to fortune.' Psychic awareness will help you to identify not only this high tide but also the low tides of life. As you progress you may well choose to follow one particular path, because there is a danger in being too eclectic and sampling too wide a variety of different approaches to the same goal. Although the essential teachings may be the same, the references and terms of definition vary, and confusion may be the result of attempting to follow too many different sets of teachings together at one time.

CHOOSING A PATH

In my own case, after very careful study I have chosen to follow the path laid down by The Aetherius Society and have found it to be of untold benefit to my life. At the same time I always keep an open mind about other systems and metaphysical philosophy in general, and make a point of studying as wide a range of teaching as possible. I have found that this does not in any way take me from the path I have chosen, but only serves to strengthen it.

Whichever road a person treads, an awareness is growing among many peoples from different religious and cultural backgrounds that all paths, in fact, lead to the same destination. The nineteenth-century Hindu Saint, Sri Ramakrishna, gave one of the most brilliantly simple parables I have ever heard. He said that if you were to blindfold eight boys, and take each one into the presence of an elephant for the first time, and then let each boy touch that elephant in a different place, you would get eight completely different descriptions of the same elephant. He said that God is just like this. Some of the great religious personalities of history have had a dim glimpse of an aspect of God, but no one has seen the whole. We all make different observations and descriptions from our own experiences, but none of them alters the fundamentally unchanged existence of God.

THE AGE OF AQUARIUS

Astrologers believe that approximately every two thousand years a different Age or Cycle ends and a new one begins. Two thousand years ago, at the time of the birth of Jesus Christ on our world, the Age of Pisces dawned. This Age has been associated with the expression of emotion, which in its most elevated and controlled form is love. Astrologers point to the fact that this all-embracing love was demonstrated in a most wonderful way by Jesus Christ, who came to herald in this Age. Irrespective of whether we regard ourselves as Christians, everything we know of Jesus points to His immense self-sacrificing capacity for loving all people, regardless of their background or status in life. Perhaps this is why He is revered not only in the Christian religion but in many others as well.

The year 2000 (approximately) according to astrologers marks the beginning of a new Cycle or Age, namely the Age of Aquarius. Much has been written, spoken and even sung about the dawning of this Age. It is a well-known idea among believers and disbelievers in astrology alike, but few people know what it really means.

Incidentally, those who are familiar with astrology may have noted that normally Pisces follows Aquarius in the astrological calendar, whereas the Age of Aquarius follows the Age of Pisces. This is because it is universally agreed among astrologers that the calculation of cycles or ages takes the signs of the zodiac in the reverse order of their normal progression through the calendar.

This coming Age will be very much associated with the mind, because Aquarius is one of the 'air signs' which govern the mental faculties of man. Astrologers say it will be an age of science, but because of the open-mindedness associated with the Aquarian sign, it should be an undogmatic type of science. Some predict that the dogmatic laws associated with orthodox science will be replaced by a willingness first to observe events and then try to understand them, rather than attempting to discover laws and then trying to make events comply with them, as so often happens in science at present.

Included in this new open-minded approach to science will be, according to the forecasts of astrologers, a readiness to accept the so-called paranormal, and regard it as perfectly normal. The study of psychic events will form an essential part of scientific discovery.

As well as science, a new open-mindedness should emerge in religion. According to the Aquarian influence, a free-thinking logic will be applied more than ever before to all world religions. Increasingly the barriers between religions will be broken down and a new unity will emerge. There should be a move away from materialistic thinking and a move towards a more altruistic approach to life.

As well as being associated with the mental attributes of man, the sign of Aquarius is also linked with the concept of universal co-operation. Astrologers therefore see the coming Age as a time of brotherhood, during which barriers of race, colour, class and creed will gradually disappear. Increasingly, religions and cultures will be seen as coming from one Universal Source, instead of being separate dogmas, each one precluding the others.

During this Age, ancient texts and documents will be re-examined without prejudice, and those man-made dogmas which have been added to them, arguably for political and financial purposes, will be stripped away from world religion, science and philosophy, leaving only the core beliefs for all to share. It will then be seen, say the most optimistic of astrological prophets, just how similar are all these beliefs in essence. This will make it possible for the beginnings of a Brotherhood of Man to emerge throughout the world.

One change which all agree will come as this Age approaches is an acceptance of ESP. This change has already started. It is commonplace nowadays to hear people talking about vibrations or 'vibes'. When visiting a building, town or even country, many people comment on the vibrations of the place and whether or not they like them. Sometimes this feeling is the first thing they experience and comment upon, before examining anything else about the place they have visited. This type of experience is symptomatic of the beginning of a change towards Aquarian Age thinking, which will not be based on rational deduction alone, although that will always be an important aspect of it, but also on those inner feelings and impressions which very often turn out to be correct.

Psychic development leads to an enhanced appreciation of all life. At the same time it is constantly teaching us something about ourselves and our own potential. There is an ancient Tibetan maxim that until you fully attain something yourself, you are not in a position to teach it to others. A western version of this would probably be that you must practise what you preach. So as someone who still has far to go on the journey towards self-realisation, I shall leave it at that—save to say that the signs of destiny are there for us all to see. When you do start to see them, even if dimly, you will know that, at least to some extent, you have unlocked your psychic powers!

Appendix

*

The following are some pointers to guide you towards a safe and effective programme of psychic development:

DO	DO NOT
Practise regularly	Dabble in the 'black arts'
Maintain control at all times	Enter a negative trance condition
Study carefully the system you choose to practise	
Learn to discriminate	Deliberately blank out your mind
Be cautious in your interpretation if you are not sure	Take hallucinogenic drugs or other stimulants
Follow a healthy life-style	Practise psychic development while you are in any way psychologically disturbed
Practise psychic development in a clean environment	Jump to hasty conclusions about psychic impressions
Practise a balanced system of breathing exercises	Allow your emotions to interfere with your psychic impressions

Develop self-confidence, but always with humility and a sense of humour

Adopt a positive approach to life

Use psychic powers to help others

Use psychic powers to heal others

Adopt a fatalistic approach to divination

Use psychic powers solely to make money or for entertainment

Use psychic powers to harm others

Notes

*

CHAPTER ONE

1 *Raja Yoga* by Swami Vivekananda. Advaita Ashrama, Himalayas, 1970.
2 *The Serpent Power* by Sir John Woodroffe (occasional penname Arthur Avalon). Dover Publications Inc., 1974.
3 Personal Development Cassettes by His Eminence Dr George King. The Aetherius Society.

CHAPTER THREE

1 *The I Ching*, translated by Richard Wilhelm. Routledge & Kegan Paul, 1951.

CHAPTER FOUR

1 *The Chakras* by C. W. Leadbeater. The Theosophical Publishing House, 1927.

CHAPTER SIX

1 The Cassette Lectures of His Eminence Dr George King. The Aetherius Society.

CHAPTER SEVEN

1 *Nature's Finer Forces* by Rama Prasad, MA. The Theosophical Publishing Society, 1897.
2 *The Kingdom of the Gods* by Geoffrey Hodson. The Theosophical Publishing House, 1952.
3 *You Too Can Heal* by George King, DD. The Aetherius Society, 1976.
4 *Autobiography of a Yogi* by Paramhansa Yogananda. Rider & Co., 1950.
5 *Contact Your Higher Self Through Yoga* by George King, DD. The Aetherius Society, 1955.
6 *The Science of Breath* by Yogi Ramacharaka. L. N. Fowler & Co., 1960.
7 I recommend the Radionic Pendulum which is manufactured by The Aetherius Society.

CHAPTER EIGHT

1 *Karma and Reincarnation* by George King, DD. The Aetherius Society, 1962.
2 *The Tibetan Book of the Dead*, edited W. Y. Evans-Wentz. Oxford University Press, 1927.
3 *The Egyptian Book of the Dead*, translated and edited by Sir Wallis Budge. Routledge & Kegan Paul, 1909.

CHAPTER TEN

1 *The Science of the Sacraments* by C. W. Leadbeater. The Theosophical Publishing House, 1920.

Recommended Reading

*

In addition to the publications listed in the notes, and numerous others which have been studied by the author in researching this subject, the following books have provided an invaluable source of reference:

George King, DD. *The Nine Freedoms*. The Aetherius Society, 1963.
Mabel Collins. *Light on the Path*. Theosophical Publishing House, 1972.
W. Y. Evans-Wentz. *The Tibetan Book of The Great Liberation*. Oxford University Press, 1954.
Swami Sivananda. *Concentration and Meditation*. Divine Life Society, 1954.

There are many courses available on personal development. Those run by The Aetherius Society College of Spiritual Sciences are particularly recommended.

If you wish to receive further information or advice, please contact:

The Aetherius Society, 6202 Afton Place, Hollywood, California 90028-8298.

Index